KURT VONNEGUT

Critical Companions to Popular Contemporary Writers
Second Series

KURT VONNEGUT

A Critical Companion

Thomas F. Marvin

CRITICAL COMPANIONS TO POPULAR CONTEMPORARY WRITERS
Kathleen Gregory Klein, Series Editor

Greenwood Press
Westport, Connecticut • London

Library of Congress Cataloging-in-Publication Data

Marvin, Thomas F.
    Kurt Vonnegut—a critical companion / Thomas F. Marvin.
      p. cm.—(Critical companions to popular contemporary writers, ISSN 1082-4979)
    Includes bibliographical references.
    ISBN 0-313-31439-X (alk. paper)
    1. Vonnegut, Kurt—Criticism and interpretation.   2. Science fiction, American—
History and criticism.   I. Title.   II. Series.
    PS3572.O5Z766   2002
    813'.54—dc21   2001054544

British Library Cataloguing in Publication Data is available.

Library of Congress Catalog Card Number: 2001054544
ISBN: 0-313-31439-X
ISSN: 1082-4979

First published in 2002

Greenwood Press, 88 Post Road West, Westport, CT 06881
An imprint of Greenwood Publishing Group, Inc.
www.greenwood.com

Printed in the United States of America

∞

The paper used in this book complies with the
Permanent Paper Standard issued by the National
Information Standards Organization (Z39.48–1984).

10 9 8 7 6 5 4 3 2 1

Contents

Series Foreword

The authors who appear in the series Critical Companions to Popular Contemporary Writers are all best-selling writers. They do not simply have one successful novel, but a string of them. Fans, critics, and specialist readers eagerly anticipate their next book. For some, high cash advances and breakthrough sales figures are automatic; movie deals often follow. Some writers become household names, recognized by almost everyone.

But, their novels are read one by one. Each reader chooses to start and, more importantly, to finish a book because of what she or he finds there. The real test of a novel is in the satisfaction its readers experience. This series acknowledges the extraordinary involvement of readers and writers in creating a best-seller.

The authors included in this series were chosen by an Advisory Board composed of high school English teachers and high school and public librarians. They ranked a list of best-selling writers according to their popularity among different groups of readers. For the first series, writers in the top-ranked group who had received no book-length, academic, literary analysis (or none in at least the past ten years) were chosen. Because of this selection method, Critical Companions to Popular Contemporary Writers meets a need that is being addressed nowhere else. The success of these volumes as reported by reviewers, librarians, and teachers led to an expansion of the series mandate to include some writers with wide critical attention—Toni Morrison, John Irving, and Maya Angelou, for example—to extend the usefulness of the series.

The volumes in the series are written by scholars with particular expertise in analyzing popular fiction. These specialists add an academic focus to the popular success that these writers already enjoy.

The series is designed to appeal to a wide range of readers. The general reading public will find explanations for the appeal of these well-known writers. Fans will find biographical and fictional questions answered. Students will find literary analysis, discussions of fictional genres, carefully organized introductions to new ways of reading the novels, and bibliographies for additional research. Whether browsing through the book for pleasure or using it for an assignment, readers will find that the most recent novels of the authors are included.

Each volume begins with a biographical chapter drawing on published information, autobiographies or memoirs, prior interviews, and, in some cases, interviews given especially for this series. A chapter on literary history and genres describes how the author's work fits into a larger literary context. The following chapters analyze the writer's most important, most popular, and most recent novels in detail. Each chapter focuses on one or more novels. This approach, suggested by the advisory board as the most useful to student research, allows for an in-depth analysis of the writer's fiction. Close and careful readings with numerous examples show readers exactly how the novels work. These chapters are organized around three central elements: plot development (how the story line moves forward), character development (what the reader knows of the important figures), and theme (the significant ideas of the novel). Chapters may also include sections on generic conventions (how the novel is similar to or different from others in its same category of science fiction, fantasy, thriller, etc.), narrative point of view (who tells the story and how), symbols and literary language, and historical or social context. Each chapter ends with an "alternative reading" of the novel. The volume concludes with a primary and secondary bibliography, including reviews.

The alternative readings are a unique feature of this series. By demonstrating a particular way of reading each novel, they provide a clear example of how a specific perspective can reveal important aspects of the book. In the alternative reading sections, one contemporary literary theory—way of reading, such as feminist criticism, Marxism, new historicism, deconstruction, or Jungian psychological critique—is defined in brief, easily comprehensible language. That definition is then applied to the novel to highlight specific features that might go unnoticed or be understood differently in a more general reading. Each volume defines two or three specific theories, making them part of the reader's understanding of how diverse meanings may be constructed from a single novel.

Taken collectively, the volumes in the Critical Companions to Popular Contemporary Writers series provide a wide-ranging investigation of the complexities of current best-selling fiction. By treating these novels seriously as both literary works and publishing successes, the series demonstrates the potential of popular literature in contemporary culture.

Kathleen Gregory Klein
Southern Connecticut State University

1

The Life of Kurt Vonnegut

Kurt Vonnegut is one of the most prolific and popular writers of the twentieth century. His career has spanned fifty years and brought him prestigious awards and honorary degrees from many universities. Although his novels have sometimes come under savage attack from professional critics, an impressive and ever growing list of academic studies suggests that his reputation as one of the most important American novelists of the twentieth century is secure. Since the late 1960s, he has been a public figure, speaking out on issues ranging from politics to censorship, from science and technology to the role of the artist in modern society. His face has become familiar, even to those who have never read his books or heard him give a commencement address, from his appearances in movies and television advertisements. Readers often become "addicted" to Vonnegut, devouring his books one after another and becoming curious about the man who wrote them. Vonnegut has provided plenty of clues about the connection between his life and work by weaving autobiographical details into his fiction and discussing the process of writing novels in the novels themselves. In countless interviews he has examined the major influences that shaped his life and career. In addition, three collections of shorter works, *Wampeters, Foma, & Granfalloons; Palm Sunday*; and *Fates Worse than Death*, contain many interesting and revealing anecdotes that help readers understand the man behind the novels. This chapter will draw on interviews and Vonnegut's own autobiographical essays to provide a brief overview of his life and explore the connections between his experiences and his writing.

Kurt Vonnegut, Jr., was born to Kurt Vonnegut, Sr., and Edith Lieber Vonnegut in Indianapolis, Indiana, on November 11, 1922, the fourth anniversary of the armistice that ended World War I. The coincidence is as significant as any that Vonnegut ever contrived in his fiction. Although his parents were third-generation Americans, they maintained close ties to Germany until the outbreak of the First World War. Vonnegut's father attended school in Germany. Both of his parents were fluent in German, and before the war they made frequent trips to Europe. In Indianapolis they were prominent members of the German-American professional and artistic elite. Vonnegut's mother Edith was born into one of the wealthiest families in town, the Liebers, who owned a successful brewery. His father was the son of a prominent architect who designed impressive buildings that still stand, including Das Deutsch Haus, the center for German culture in Indianapolis. Now known as "The Atheneum," it is included in the National Register of Historic Places. Before World War I, Vonnegut's parents lived in a world of German literature, music, and tradition, but when the United States entered the war, this world was destroyed. The United States allied itself with Britain against Germany, and almost overnight, all aspects of German culture were regarded with suspicion. German Americans were called upon to give up their ties to Germany in order to prove their patriotism. Although his parents continued to speak German to each other at home, they never taught the language to Kurt, Jr., nor did they introduce him to "the literature or the music or the oral family histories which my ancestors had loved" (*Palm Sunday* 20). This decision left Vonnegut feeling "ignorant and rootless," and throughout his work, characters suffer from a lack of connection to a vital culture and community. Both of his parents were deeply saddened by the loss of the rich cultural heritage that had sustained them before the war.

During the 1920s Vonnegut's father designed several important buildings, including a large department store, a theater, and the Indiana headquarters of the Bell Telephone Company. He also designed the telephone company's branch offices, and young Kurt sometimes rode with him to check the progress of buildings around the state (Allen, *Conversations* 243). However, the Great Depression of the 1930s put a halt to building, and Kurt, Sr., had no work from 1929 to 1940. He retreated from life and became "a dreamy artist" (Allen, *Conversations* 227). Although Kurt, Jr., defends his father's "decision to disengage" from a world that he found brutal and ugly, he regrets that his father's retreat left "very little for a son to relate to" (Allen, *Conversations* 227–28). The fathers depicted in Vonnegut's novels are all distant and uninvolved with their children's lives, reflecting Vonnegut's relationship with his own father. His first novel, *Player Piano*, explores the dehumanizing effects of a lack of meaningful work—observing his father's deepening depression during the 1930s may have suggested this theme.

Although the Vonnegut family never suffered the severe hardships that plagued many families during the Depression, they were no longer wealthy, and in 1930, Kurt, Jr., was taken out of private school and placed in Public School #43. Although Vonnegut considers this a positive development that brought him into contact with "interesting" people, his mother never recovered from the loss of the family fortune (Allen, *Conversations* 270). She became depressed and withdrew from her children's lives. For a while she tried writing short stories for popular magazines and dreamed of moving to Cape Cod, but her stories were rejected, and she became increasingly bitter and abusive. "Late at night, and always in the privacy of our own home, and never with guests present, she expressed hatred for Father as corrosive as hydrofluoric acid" (*Fates Worse than Death* 28). Although she was never diagnosed or treated, her son is convinced that she suffered from mental illness. She ended her own life with an overdose of sleeping pills on Mother's Day in 1944, while Kurt was home on leave from the army before being shipped overseas. Edith Vonnegut had voiced her strong opposition to the war, and the timing of her suicide must have burdened her son with an extra share of guilt. In Vonnegut's fiction, mothers are either distant or absent. Eliot Rosewater feels responsible for killing his mother in a sailing accident. Howard Campbell's mother is morbid and crazy before she drops out of her son's life entirely. Celia Hoover, who resembles Edith Vonnegut in several ways, commits suicide by swallowing Drano. Taken together, these fictional mothers reflect the sadness, anger, and guilt that Kurt Vonnegut has struggled with since his mother's suicide. He has tried to cope with her legacy in his life as well, fulfilling her unrealized dreams by becoming a successful short-story writer and living on Cape Cod. As he pointed out in an interview, "It's probably very common for sons to try to make their mothers' impossible dreams come true" (Allen, *Conversations* 178).

As the youngest of three children, Kurt, Jr., had to compete for attention. He soon discovered that being funny was a sure way to be noticed. His brother Bernard was nine years older and a scientist, his sister Alice was five years older and a sculptress. Along with his architect father, "they had really big time stuff to argue about" (Allen, *Conversations* 69).

But young Kurt was determined to join the conversation. "I wanted to talk in order to learn how to do it, to engage in give and take, and I must have made accidental jokes at first. Everyone does. . . . And I understood the terms under which I could buy my way into the conversations, small as I was" (Allen, *Conversations* 69). Encouraged by his success at making jokes, Kurt studied the radio comedians who were so popular during the 1930s, emulating their techniques and their timing. His ability to make jokes eventually contributed to his success as a writer. Vonnegut describes his novels as "mosaics made up of a whole bunch of tiny chips; and each chip is a joke" (Allen, *Conversations* 91).

Although his parents were distant, there were two adults who were close to Vonnegut in his childhood and helped shape his character. He describes his father's younger brother Alex as "responsive and amusing and generous with me, . . . my ideal grown-up friend" (*Palm Sunday* 53). During the 1930s, Uncle Alex was a socialist, and he introduced young Kurt to Thorstein Veblen's *Theory of the Leisure Class*. Kurt "loved it, since it made low comedy of the empty graces and aggressively useless possessions which my parents, and especially my mother, meant to regain some day" (*Palm Sunday* 54). The influence of Veblen's harsh critique of the idle rich is obvious in most of Vonnegut's work, but especially in *God Bless You, Mr. Rosewater*. Ida Young, the Vonneguts' African American cook and housekeeper during Kurt's first ten years, was also an important influence on him. Vonnegut gives Ida Young most of the credit for raising him and describes her as "humane and wise" (Allen, *Conversations* 245). He adds that she "gave me decent moral instruction and was exceedingly nice to me. So she was as great an influence on me as anybody" (Allen, *Conversations* 245). Even the most despicable characters in Vonnegut's novels are capable of arousing the reader's sympathy because they are presented as vulnerable human beings struggling to cope in a difficult world. Ms. Young also nurtured Vonnegut's capacity for sympathy. "The compassionate, forgiving aspects of my beliefs came from Ida Young."

Most high schools are lucky to produce a student newspaper several times a year, but when Vonnegut attended Shortridge High School in Indianapolis in the 1930s he worked on a daily paper, the *Shortridge Echo*. Working first as a reporter, and then as a columnist and editor, Vonnegut discovered his talent for writing. "Each person has something he can do easily and can't imagine why everybody else is having so much trouble doing it. In my case it was writing" (*Wampeters, Foma & Granfalloons* 260). Writing for a daily student newspaper made Vonnegut aware of his audience at an age when most people are writing only for their teachers.

"I started out writing for a large audience. And if I did a lousy job, I caught a lot of shit in twenty-four hours" (260). A strong sense of audience has shaped Vonnegut's writing style. He is aware that most people are not good readers, and if he hopes to hold their interest, he needs to write in a simple style with short sentences and paragraphs. "I avoid sentences where the reader could get lost. . . . I have made my books easy to read, carefully punctuated, with lots of white space" (Allen, *Conversations* 48).

When Vonnegut finished high school, he wanted to stay in Indianapolis and become a reporter for a local paper, but his father insisted that he go to college and study chemistry. Kurt began his freshman year at Cornell University in Ithaca, New York, in 1940 as a biochemistry major. Although by then his older brother Bernard was well on his way to a promising career as a scientist, Kurt soon realized that he had little scientific ability. He spent most of his college years writing for the *Cornell Daily Sun*, a student-run newspaper. As managing editor of the *Sun*, Vonnegut wrote three columns a week that he describes as "impudent editorializing, . . . college-humor sort of stuff" (Allen, *Conversations* 114). Vonnegut enjoyed the opportunity to express his opinions in an amusing way in his editorials, and he has continued this practice in his novels. "I've always had to have an ax to grind in order to write" (Allen, *Conversations* 114). After three years at Cornell, Vonnegut had polished his prose style, but he was flunking most of his science classes. Although he never received a degree from Cornell, his scientific training proved valuable to his career as a novelist. He learned enough about science to discuss it intelligently, to admire the work of scientists, and to assess technology's impact on society. He even adopted a modified "scientific" approach to his writing. Vonnegut points out that scientists like his brother Bernard are always asking "what if" questions and then designing experiments to answer them. Vonnegut does the same thing in his fiction by creating unlikely situations to see what they reveal about human nature. These mind experiments challenge readers to think more deeply about the world around them and their place in it.

Because he was about to flunk out of Cornell in his junior year, Vonnegut was "delighted to join the Army and go to war" (Allen, *Conversations* 181). He was trained to fire the army's largest piece of field artillery, the 240 mm howitzer, an enormous cannon that shot a 300-pound shell. But before he was shipped overseas, he was transferred to the 106th Infantry Division as a battalion scout. Vonnegut received no infantry training, because "nobody was very sure" about what battalion scouts were supposed to do (*Palm Sunday* 76). When he found himself at the front, he "imitated various war movies [he] had seen" (77). During the Battle of the Bulge, the largest American defeat of the Second World War, Vonnegut was captured by the Germans. Although he could not speak German well, he knew a few words from listening to his parents, and he tried to speak to his captors. They asked him if he was of German heritage and then wanted to know why he was fighting against his "brothers." Vonnegut found the question "ignorant and comical. My parents had separated me so thoroughly from my Germanic past that my captors might as well have been Bolivians or Tibetans, for all they meant to me" (78–79).

As a prisoner of war, Vonnegut was shipped to Dresden, a beautiful city that had so far been spared by the Allied bombing. As the son and grandson of architects, Vonnegut was impressed by the ornate buildings and the city's harmonious design. He and his fellow prisoners were quartered in a slaughterhouse and put to work in a factory making malt syrup as a vitamin supplement for pregnant women. Dresden was considered an "open" city, meaning there were no war industries or large troop concentrations there, so its residents believed that they would not be bombed. However, on the night of February 13, 1945, the air raid sirens wailed, and Dresdeners retreated to their cellars. Vonnegut and the other prisoners descended to an underground meat locker, where the carcasses of animals hung in the cool air. When they emerged a few hours later, the beautiful city of Dresden had been reduced to a pile of smoking rubble, and 135,000 people were dead. It was the largest massacre in European history. British and American planes dropped thousands of incendiary devices on Dresden and created a firestorm that destroyed the entire city and suffocated the Dresdeners in their cellars. Vonnegut and his fellow prisoners survived because they were far enough under ground that the air was not sucked out of their shelter by the firestorm. Afterward, Vonnegut was put to work as a "corpse miner," excavating the cellars of Dresden to remove the dead and bring them to the city's parks where enormous funeral pyres burned the bodies to prevent the spread of disease. Vonnegut's wartime experiences provided the basis for his most famous and important novel, *Slaughterhouse-Five*.

After the war, Vonnegut returned briefly to Indianapolis and married his high-school sweetheart, Jane Marie Cox, on September 1, 1945. When he first got home, she was engaged to another man, but Vonnegut persuaded her to go for a walk with him and then convinced her to marry him instead. This incident later became the basis for one of Vonnegut's first published stories, "Long Walk to Forever," which appeared in the *Ladies Home Journal* and was later included in a collection of Vonnegut's stories, *Welcome to the Monkey House*. Vonnegut later described the story as "sickeningly slick" and lamented, "Shame, shame, to have lived scenes from a woman's magazine" (*Welcome to the Monkey House* xv). In December, the Vonneguts moved to Chicago where Kurt worked as a police reporter for the Chicago City News Bureau, a company that supplied local news stories to the Chicago newspapers and the national wire services. He also began studying for a master's degree in anthropology at the University of Chicago. For the first time since high school, Vonnegut enjoyed his studies. He specialized in cultural anthropology, which he describes as the study of "every object and idea which has been shaped by men and women and children" (*Palm Sunday* 222). His choice of anthropology reveals that he was still under the influence of his father's advice to study a science, even as he gained a clearer idea of his real talents. For Vonnegut, anthropology was "a science that was mostly poetry" (90). Cultural anthropology showed Vonnegut that people in other parts of the world had worked out patterns for living that were quite different from anything he had been exposed to in his first twenty-three years of life. Although he found his studies interesting, and he eventually put his new knowledge to good use in his novels, the anthropology department rejected his master's thesis, and he left Chicago without a degree in 1947. Twenty-five years later, a professor read Vonnegut's novel *Cat's Cradle* and showed it to his colleagues in anthropology, who voted to accept it as Vonnegut's master's thesis. He was awarded a Master of Arts degree in anthropology by the University of Chicago in 1971. The rejected thesis, "Fluctuations Between Good and Evil in Simple Tales," later became a regular feature of his public lectures, and a summary of it was finally published in *Palm Sunday* (1981). Writing it helped Vonnegut understand some simple but important truths about storytelling that he was soon to put to good use.

In 1947 Vonnegut was broke, he had only a high school diploma, and he needed to find work to support his wife and his young son Mark. By now his older brother Bernard was working in General Electric's research laboratories in Schenectady, New York, and he got Kurt a job in public relations. Because he had some training in science, Vonnegut was assigned to write articles about the research being done in GE's labs. Although he found the company of the scientists interesting, he hated his job and felt out of place at GE. He began writing short stories at night, and after a few rejections, he sold his first story, "Report on the Barnhouse Effect," to *Collier's* for $750, which was the equivalent of six weeks' pay at GE. His next story brought him $950, and he decided to quit his job to write full time. Vonnegut regards the four years he spent at GE as a period of apprenticeship, during which he received instruction in the craft of writing stories from the magazine editors who purchased his work. In Schenectady he was surrounded by engineers and machinery, and they became the focus of his first novel, *Player Piano*. *Cat's Cradle* is also based on Vonnegut's experiences at GE, and throughout his career, Vonnegut has written about the role of science and technology in the modern world.

After quitting his job at GE in 1951, Vonnegut moved to West Barnstable, Massachusetts, a scenic coastal town on Cape Cod. There he continued to write short stories to pay the bills as he worked on his novel *Player Piano*, which was published in 1952. As his family continued to grow with the births of Edith in 1951 and Nanette in 1955, Vonnegut needed to supplement the income he received from his stories. He taught English for one year at the Hopefield School in nearby Sandwich, Massachusetts, worked for an industrial advertising agency, and opened the second Saab automobile dealership in the United States. In the late 1950s he even created a large metal sculpture that was on display in the lobby of a hotel at Logan airport in Boston for over ten years (Todd 17).

In 1957 Vonnegut's father died alone in a small cottage in the woods of southern Indiana. Although he and Kurt, Jr., had never been close, his death marked a decisive severing of Vonnegut's Indiana roots. Although Indianapolis is mentioned in all of Vonnegut's novels, since his father's death he has returned to his hometown only for funerals and an occasional speaking engagement. He laments the loss of the city's distinctive culture, complaining that now it is no more than "an interchangeable part in the American machine" (*Slapstick* 8). Yet the city of his youth remains an important influence on Vonnegut's writing. "I myself find that I trust my own writing most, and others seem to trust it most too, when I sound like a person from Indianapolis, which is what I am" (*Palm Sunday* 70).

Less than a year after his father's death, Vonnegut's beloved sister Alice died of cancer, leaving behind four young boys. The day before she died, her husband, James Carmalt Adams, was killed in a train wreck on the way to visit her in the hospital. Although Vonnegut has not said much about his relationship with his sister, she was certainly an important influence on his life and work. "I . . . never told her so, but she was the person I had always written for. She was the secret of whatever artistic unity I had ever achieved. She was the secret of my technique" (*Slapstick* 16–17). His novel *Slapstick* "depicts myself and my beautiful sister as monsters" whose parents have abandoned them in a house full of books (20). The "monsters" are described as "specialized halves of a single brain," suggesting the close, creative relationship that Vonnegut enjoyed with his sister. After her death, he and his wife Jane adopted her three oldest boys, James, Steven, and Kurt Adams.

Now there were six children between the ages of nine and fourteen in the Vonnegut household on Cape Cod, and Kurt was faced with the dual challenge of providing for them and guiding them through their teenage years in the 1960s. Unfortunately, the magazines that Vonnegut relied on to buy his stories were going out of business, so he began selling his novels to paperback publishers, who would give him a $3,000 advance based on an outline and a first chapter. The money enabled him to feed his large family, but paperback originals are rarely reviewed and are sold mostly in bus stations and drug stores, so they did little to enhance Vonnegut's reputation as a writer. *The Sirens of Titan, Mother Night*, and *Canary in a Cathouse*, a collection of stories, were all published first in paperback. "*Cat's Cradle* was written with that market in mind," Vonnegut recalls, but it was published in hardcover in 1963. Before the success of *Cat's Cradle*, Vonnegut felt that his work was being ignored. "I wasn't even getting reviewed. *Esquire* published a list of the American literary world back then and it guaranteed that every living author of the slightest merit was on there somewhere. I wasn't on there . . . [and] it made me feel subhuman" (Allen, *Conversations* 107). Vonnegut's frustration with being relegated to the "sleazo" world of paperback originals is reflected in one of his most memorable characters, Kilgore Trout, the prolific science fiction writer whose novels can be found only in pornographic bookstores.

When his novels began to appear in hardcover, Vonnegut received the critical recognition he desired, but he still struggled to make ends meet. In spite of the fact that both *Cat's Cradle* and *God Bless You, Mr. Rosewater* received favorable reviews, they soon went out of print, and by 1965, Vonnegut was having difficulty supporting his large family. He was offered a teaching position at the prestigious University of Iowa Writers' Workshop, so he moved his family to Iowa City for two years between 1965 and 1967. For the first time in his life, Vonnegut was part of a community of writers, and he found the experience exhilarating yet intimidating. Because his education was in science, he had not read many of the great novels that his new colleagues were fond of discussing, so he went on a crash course in reading. For the first time in his life, he was expected to talk about writing, which forced him to think more deeply about his own creative process. During these years, Vonnegut was struggling to write about his wartime experiences in Dresden, and he found it helpful to be able to discuss his work with other writers. His training as a journalist had taught him to keep himself out of his writing as much as possible, but the fiction writers at Iowa told him that this rule does not apply to fiction. Vonnegut found this advice liberating. He wrote an autobiographical introduction to the hardcover reissue of *Mother Night* and began to write first-person accounts of his wartime experiences for *Slaughterhouse-Five*, signaling a new direction in his work.

In 1967 Vonnegut was awarded a prestigious Guggenheim fellowship to travel to Dresden to do research for *Slaughterhouse-Five*. Of course, the city bore no resemblance to the architectural treasure that it had been before the war. It reminded Vonnegut of Dayton, Ohio. The Germans Vonnegut met were not eager to recall their wartime experiences, nor were his fellow prisoners. Most found they could recall little about the period, and Vonnegut faced the same problem when he sat down to write a book about Dresden. He felt he had to do it, but he did not know how. Only after years of struggle and many abandoned drafts did he finally succeed in completing *Slaughterhouse-Five*. The novel was a best-seller, and it brought Vonnegut financial security and praise from the critics. Published at the height of the Vietnam War, it demonstrated that aerial bombardment is a purposeless slaughter of innocents with no military justification. Vonnegut became a hero of the anti-war movement. He was invited to speak at rallies, to teach at Harvard, and to give commencement addresses at colleges all over the country.

At the same time, his twenty-five-year marriage was falling apart. Vonnegut described the break-up as a "terrible, unavoidable accident that we were ill-equipped to understand" (*Palm Sunday* 172). Five of their six children were grown and out on their own, and this meant that "[w]e were both going to have to find other sorts of seemingly important work to do." Vonnegut and his wife Jane also fought about religion. She was becoming a born-again Christian, and Vonnegut, a life-long atheist, found this "painful" (175). So in 1971 he left their home on Cape Cod and moved to New York City, although he and Jane remained friends until the end of her life.

The combination of financial security and emotional distress took a toll on Vonnegut's writing. "I am in the dangerous position now where I can sell anything I write," he explained to an interviewer in 1971 (Todd 17). Yet he was deeply disappointed with his progress on his next novel, *Breakfast of Champions*. He abandoned it for a while and began to think seriously of a new career as a playwright. Staging plays gave him a chance to join an interesting community and leave behind the loneliness of the solitary writer. "I write for the stage in order to get to know more people and to become intimately related to them" (Allen, *Conversations*

71). *Happy Birthday, Wanda June* opened at the Theatre de Lys in New York on October 7, 1970, and ran until March 14, in spite of mixed reviews. Vonnegut thoroughly enjoyed the experience of working with the actors, but he soon realized that his true talent was for writing fiction.

Throughout the 1970s, Vonnegut received many honors and awards. He taught at Harvard and at City University of New York, where he was the Distinguished Professor of English Prose. He was elected vice president of the National Institute of Arts and Letters, and he received honorary degrees from Indiana University, Hobart and William College, and Bennington College, among others. In 1972 Universal Pictures released a film adaptation of *Slaughterhouse-Five* that Vonnegut called "flawless" (*Between Time and Timbuktu* xv). Yet in spite of his growing fame, Vonnegut was facing an artistic crisis. *Slaughterhouse-Five* was a book that he felt compelled to write, but after it was finished, he did not know what to do next. When *Breakfast of Champions* appeared in 1973, critics viciously attacked it, and Vonnegut's reputation continued to slide with the publication of *Slapstick* in 1976. Critics were not content to say that these were bad books. They felt compelled to attack the author and suggest that he had no business writing at all. "All of a sudden critics wanted me squashed like a bug" (*Palm Sunday* 93). Vonnegut had never been part of the literary establishment. He had not attended a prestigious East Coast prep school and gone on to study literature at an Ivy League college, as many of his critics had. Although he always felt like an outsider, the interviews he gave in the 1970s reveal that he was deeply hurt by the personal nature of the critics' attacks. "The hidden complaint was that I was barbarous, that I wrote without having made a systematic study of the great literature, that I was no gentleman, since I had done hack writing so cheerfully for vulgar magazines" (93–94).

The seventies were also a difficult decade in Vonnegut's personal life. His son Mark suffered a mental breakdown in 1972, and Vonnegut had to put him in an institution. Although Mark recovered and wrote a book about the experience, *The Eden Express*, his illness was deeply troubling and contributed to Vonnegut's own chronic depression. For a while he took Ritalin, a prescription anti-depressant, and was amazed that a little pill could do so much to change his mood. In the mid-seventies, he stopped taking it and began having weekly talks with a psychologist. These talks helped him put an end to the "periodic blowups" that had afflicted him since childhood (*Wampeters, Foma & Granfalloons* 253). Vonnegut also considers his writing important therapy. "Writers are very lucky people, they can treat their neuroses every day" (Abel A11). Lawrence Broer has argued convincingly that in his novels of the seventies and eighties, Vonnegut attempted to come to terms with the psychic pain that his parents had inflicted on him as a child.

In the early 1970s, Vonnegut met Jill Krementz, a photojournalist who was working on a series about writers at work. They lived together in New York and were married in 1979. Vonnegut has had less to say about his personal life in the last twenty years, but he seems pleased to be a grandfather and to have all of his books in print. Two novels that he published in the 1980s, *Galapagos* and *Bluebeard*, have helped to restore his reputation as a major writer. Vonnegut played himself in the 1986 Rodney Dangerfield movie *Back to School*, making his face familiar to a whole new generation of readers.

Vonnegut still loves to stir up controversy, especially when he suspects that people are in danger of taking themselves too seriously. Recently he completed a year as writer-in-residence at Smith College in Northampton, Massachusetts. In a public lecture he confessed his lust for an Indian woman and wondered aloud if she soaks the jewel she wears on her forehead at night, like a set of dentures. The remark prompted an angry editorial in the school newspaper, claiming that students "would have walked out on anyone else who uttered the same things" (quoted in Abel A11). By now Vonnegut is used to such criticism, and he laughs it off easily. The remark is another Vonnegut mind experiment, intended to make people think more deeply about who they are and how they see the world. He knows full well that his statement is not "politically correct," but he insists that we must be able to speak frankly about sensitive subjects without becoming too afraid that we will offend someone else in the process. "I'll say whatever I want; that's the price of my freedom. If it hurts someone's feelings, too bad! That's the way it goes" (Abel A11).

As he approaches his eightieth birthday, Vonnegut is still writing full time and seeking other outlets for his creativity. While in Northampton he has given poetry readings, done some stand-up comedy, sung with a band he called "Special K and his Crew" and presented his visual art in a local gallery. The working title for his novel-in-progress is *If God Were Alive Today*. He still chain-smokes Pall Mall cigarettes, as he has since the age of fourteen, but now he is contemplating a lawsuit against the tobacco companies. "They promised to kill me on the package, and they haven't done it yet" (Abel A11). He still believes that laughter is the best response to a world filled with pain and horror. In spite of all he has been through, he feels that he "got off so *light*" (Reed & Leeds ix). In 1999 he insisted that he still wants his gravestone carved with the words that appealed to Billy Pilgrim in *Slaughterhouse-Five*: "Everything was beautiful, and nothing hurt."

2

Literary Contexts

At different stages of his career, Kurt Vonnegut's writing has been categorized as science fiction, satire, black humor, and postmodern. All of these labels are limiting and none does justice to the range of Vonnegut's fiction, but an understanding of each one provides literary contexts for his novels and helps readers appreciate an aspect of his literary achievements.

Early in his career, Vonnegut was considered a science fiction writer because his first two novels were set in the future and included space ships, super computers, and other technological gadgets. Science fiction was very popular in the 1950s when Vonnegut began writing, and it remains so today. To boost sales, his publishers emphasized the science fiction elements of his novels by adorning their covers with space ships and Martian colonies. They even changed the title of *Player Piano* to *Utopia-14* to make it sound more like a conventional science fiction novel. In a limited sense, the science fiction label is appropriate for much of Vonnegut's work because of his persistent interest in technology and the future of mankind, but he does not consider himself a science fiction writer. Instead, he argues that all writers need to learn more about science because it has become such an important part of human life. Vonnegut also objects to the "science fiction" label because it is often used as a way of refusing to take writers seriously. "The feeling persists that no one can simultaneously be a respectable writer and understand how a refrigerator works" (*Wampeters, Foma & Granfalloons* 1). Most literary critics will not admit to reading science fiction, but if they are pressed for an opinion, they are likely to say that it is all poorly written hack work intended to fill the pages of the pulp magazines that appeal to adolescent boys. Being called a "science fiction writer" is the kiss of death for anyone who hopes to have his or her novels taken seriously.

Another problem with the science fiction label is that people cannot seem to agree on just what it means. An interest in technology and the future is assumed, but what else serves to link writers as diverse as Isaac Asimov, Arthur C. Clark, Ray Bradbury, Philip K. Dick, Aldous Huxley, and Vonnegut? Putting all of these authors in the same file drawer and labeling it "science fiction" does little to help us understand their individual works. All it really does is place them in the broad context of writers who have responded imaginatively to the increasing importance of science and technology in the modern world.

Following the lead of Aldous Huxley's *Brave New World*, Vonnegut uses the conventions of science fiction to force his readers to think more deeply about the world we actually live in. Like Huxley, Vonnegut is not interested in high-tech gadgets for their own sake, nor does he describe future civilizations merely to excite his readers. Instead he imagines other worlds because they allow him to point out what is wrong with contemporary society. Seen in this light, Vonnegut becomes part of the older tradition of satire, where new worlds are imagined in order to criticize our own. The tradition of satire goes all the way back to the ancient Greeks. Satires often present their readers with a world that resembles the one they live in, except that certain aspects of it are exaggerated for comic effect. The animated television show *The Simpsons* provides a good example of this technique. Because it is a cartoon, the show is obviously removed from everyday reality, yet the characters share the concerns and the petty vices of millions of contemporary Americans. Successful satirists must balance realism and exaggeration. Like Jonathan Swift in *Gulliver's Travels*, Vonnegut imagines future worlds and distant places not for their own sake, but for the power they give him to point out what is wrong back home.

Satires poke fun at human failings, make readers laugh at the absurdities of their own societies, and turn that laughter into a weapon in the battle to improve the human condition. Satirists believe that if people can be made to see, and laugh at, their own faults and the injustices of society, they will be inspired to work toward reform. Although the aim of satire is serious, the tone is light because it relies on laughter as its principal weapon.

Over the centuries, satire has developed certain conventions that distinguish it from other genres. Satire rarely criticizes individuals. Instead it makes fun of recognizable human types. In the case of *The Simpsons*, these types include the lazy beer-drinking slob, the corrupt politician, and the greedy and ruthless millionaire. Because they are meant to represent whole classes of people, characters in a satire are usually not well-developed individuals. Critics have frequently pointed out that Vonnegut does not create well-rounded characters, and, with a few notable exceptions (including Howard W. Campbell, Jr., in *Mother Night* and Rabo Karabekian in *Bluebeard*), this is a fair assessment. However, if readers are aware that they are reading satire rather than realistic, character-driven fiction, this is not a fault but rather to be expected. Satirists are not interested in making readers care about their characters or imagine that they know them intimately because this would defeat the purpose of satire, which is to make us take a cold, hard look at human failings.

Although Vonnegut's work exhibits most of the qualities of satire, he also rejects this label. When asked if his work is satire, he responds that he is not sure what satire is. "I've never even bothered to look it up. I wouldn't know whether I'm a satirist or not" (Bryan 2). This answer reflects Vonnegut's stubborn desire to resist categorization, as well as his public image as a literary outsider who is reluctant to engage in critical games. In *Fabulation and Metafiction*, critic Robert Scholes attempts to categorize Vonnegut's work and makes many astute observations in the process. Scholes points out that although Vonnegut pokes fun at social problems, he "reject[s] the traditional satirist's faith in the efficacy of satire as a reforming instrument. [He has] a more subtle faith in the humanizing value of laughter" (145). Vonnegut's own statements support this view. He is disappointed that powerful people do not read his books, or many other books for that matter, but his teaching experience has convinced him that writing can still have an impact on the world. "[Y]ou catch people before they become generals and presidents and so forth and you poison their minds with . . . humanity . . . to encourage them to make a better world" (Klinkowitz and Somer 105). Even though he does not expect that his work will improve society immediately, Vonnegut remains optimistic that in the long run it will contribute to a gradual improvement by teaching people to be more humane.

Rather than providing an escape from the harsh realities of life, Vonnegut's humor forces readers to confront the pain and suffering that humans inflict on one another. In the 1960s, novelist and critic Bruce Friedman wrote a book called *Black Humor* that lumped together several contemporary authors, including Vonnegut. Friedman argued that Terry

Southern (*Dr. Strangelove*), John Barth (*The Floating Opera*), Joseph Heller (*Catch-22*), Vonnegut, and others could be considered "black humorists" because they encourage their readers to laugh at hopeless situations. But while Friedman presents black humor as a new phenomenon, Vonnegut points out that it was common in Europe for centuries before Sigmund Freud gave it the name "gallows humor." Freud called it gallows humor because many of his examples involved condemned prisoners making jokes on the way to their executions. Like any literary label, "black humor" is useful if it calls attention to a significant aspect of Vonnegut's fiction, but it is counterproductive if it encourages readers to overlook important differences between his work and that of the other so-called black humorists. As Vonnegut pointed out in an interview, the black humorists have little in common aside from their use of a form of humor that had a long tradition before Friedman coined the term. In spite of its obvious limitations, the label "black humor" does remind readers of a central truth embodied in Vonnegut's fiction: "The biggest laughs are based on the biggest disappointments and the biggest fears" (*Wampeters, Foma & Granfalloons* 258).

Vonnegut is often considered an experimental or "postmodern" writer. Although postmodernism is difficult to define precisely, it involves a reaction against the belief that science can reveal the truth about the world. Postmodernists argue that truth is not "objective," meaning that it is not out there in the world waiting to be discovered. Instead, truth is "subjective" because it depends on how different individuals look at the world, and it varies from person to person. In literature, postmodern ideas have led writers to abandon the traditional form of the novel in favor of experimental forms that show how people create their own sub-jective truths. Rather than rely on third-person narrators who supposedly provide an objective viewpoint, postmodern writers generally prefer first-person narrators who are aware of their own limited understanding of the events they describe. Postmodern novels also call attention to the fact that they are novels by commenting on the writing process and reminding their readers that they are reading a novel, not getting a glimpse of real life. However, even as they critique traditional forms, postmodern novels create new ones and contribute to the evolution of literary traditions.

The postmodern label calls attention to several important aspects of Vonnegut's work, but like the other labels already discussed, it does not fit precisely. In *The Sirens of Titan*, Vonnegut demonstrates the folly of human beings searching for answers to life's questions outside of them-selves. Like many of his other novels, *Sirens* shows that people are most dangerous when they think they have discovered objective truth and they try to make everyone else see the world the way they do. Like the postmodernists, Vonnegut argues that objective truth is really just an illusion and that all of our ideas about the world depend on our own individual point of view.

Many of Vonnegut's novels could be described as "experimental" because they do not adhere to the conventions established by the great nineteenth-century novelists. For example, *Breakfast of Champions* features drawings by the author that do more than merely illustrate the story. They are an integral part of the novel. *Breakfast of Champions* also includes a character named "Kurt Vonnegut" who spies on the other characters from behind mirrored sunglasses and comments on the process of writing the novel. Rather than trying to create the illusion that readers are getting a glimpse of the world as it really is, Vonnegut reminds them that everything in the novel is based on his own limited, individual, subjective understanding.

Slaughterhouse-Five introduced readers to "the telegraphic schizophrenic manner of tales of the planet Tralfamadore," and American literature has not been quite the same since. Vonnegut's writing resembles telegraphic messages because all unnecessary words are left out. Short chapters are divided up into even shorter sections and placed side-by-side without the usual connections to lead readers from one to the next. This technique forces readers to make their own connections and highlights the subjective nature of reading a Vonnegut novel. For all of these reasons, Vonnegut may be considered an experimental, postmodern writer. However, we should keep in mind that unlike other experimental writers, Vonnegut has not made a systematic study of literature in order to find his own place in the tradition. In interviews, he draws a distinction between himself and writers John Barth, Donald Barthelme, and Jorge Luis Borges, who are "responding to literary experiments of the past and are refining them" (Allen, *Conversations* 215). Vonnegut was trained as a scientist, so he "couldn't play games with [his] literary ancestors" (Allen, *Conversations* 177). Vonnegut's experiments with literary form arise out of his need to find a way to express his peculiar vision of the world. "I think it can be tremendously refreshing if a creator of literature has something on his mind other than the history of literature so far" (*Palm Sunday* 94).

In spite of these statements, Vonnegut's work has been influenced by earlier writers. He grew up in a house full of books, and he was an avid reader from an early age. In his teens, he read a lot of pulp fiction, cheap paperbacks filled with science fiction, fantasy, and action-adventure stories. But he also read some classic literature, including Aristophanes, the ancient Greek playwright (445–388 B.C.E.). Aristophanes wrote comedies that were also harsh indictments of the faults of Athenian society. Vonnegut admires Artistophanes for his carefully constructed jokes that still work after 2,400 years, as well as for his social commentary. Like Aristophanes, Vonnegut creates imaginary worlds where incredible events happen in order to make his audience see our own world in a new light. Vonnegut was originally attracted to Aristophanes when he was fourteen because he was told it was "dirty" (Allen, *Conversations* 116). Aristophanes is quite frank about sexuality and bodily functions, and Vonnegut brings a similar frankness to his novels.

Vonnegut is often compared to Mark Twain, and there are significant similarities linking their lives and work. As critic William Rodney Allen has pointed out, both come from the Midwest and draw on the American tradition of storytelling and humor. Both write satire and seem to be pessimistic about the prospects of the human race. They share a skeptical attitude toward religion and started their careers as outsiders who were only grudgingly accepted into the literary establishment after becoming popular (Allen, *Conversations* 276). Vonnegut dismisses these parallels as a "game" that he has little interest in playing, but he points out that, like Twain, he was "associated with the enemy in a major war" (Allen, *Conversations* 275–76). Twain served briefly in the Confederate army, and Vonnegut's German name links him with America's enemy in both world wars, in spite of his own service in the U.S. Army. Vonnegut speculates that the "uneasiness" of being associated with the enemy contributed to Twain's "comic energy" and that a similar uneasiness prompts him to tell jokes to placate a potentially hostile audience (*Palm Sunday* 165).

Ernest Hemingway had an enormous impact on American writing in the twentieth century, and on several occasions, Vonnegut has expressed his admiration for Hemingway's simple, direct style. Both Hemingway and Vonnegut began their careers as journalists, and this probably explains their similar writing styles better than the idea that Vonnegut consciously imitated Hemingway. Nevertheless, the similarities are there. Both writers use short, simple words and sentences and concentrate on external description of characters and events. They usually avoid any attempt to explain a character's motives. As Vonnegut points out, journalists are trained to tell "no more than you know" (Allen, *Conversations* 301). Vonnegut has also mentioned that his style results from an early decision to emulate Henry David Thoreau, who wrote in the voice of a child in order to be better understood. This childlike voice allows

Vonnegut to present his ideas with an air of innocence and simplicity that makes them more charming. As his newspaper experience taught him, a writer's first and most important task is to keep his readers reading.

Vonnegut frequently mentions Robert Louis Stevenson (1850–1894) as an important influence on his writing. Vonnegut admires Stevenson, the author of such adventures as *Treasure Island* and *The Strange Case of Dr. Jekyll and Mr. Hyde*, for his ability to tell a story that will hold the reader's interest. Vonnegut says he kept Stevenson's example in mind while he was writing for popular magazines in the 1950s. Stevenson taught him that curiosity about what will happen next is what keeps most readers going, but a skillful storyteller can maintain that curiosity and make significant comments on life at the same time.

When asked to name his favorite writer, Vonnegut often mentions George Orwell, the author of the political satires *Animal Farm* and *1984*. Orwell is the only writer that Vonnegut will admit to imitating. "I like his concern for the poor, I like his socialism, I like his simplicity" (Allen, *Conversations* 53). Vonnegut and Orwell agree that human life could be greatly improved if people would only share the world's wealth. In his famous essay "Politics and the English Language," Orwell points out how politicians misuse language to deceive people. In *God Bless You, Mr. Rosewater*, Vonnegut's Senator Rosewater uses the techniques that Orwell criticizes to convince his constituents that the rich deserve everything they have, and sharing anything with the poor will only make them lazy.

RECURRING THEMES

The unequal distribution of wealth and its harmful influence on American society and culture is one of Vonnegut's most important recurring themes. In *The Sirens of Titan*, Malachi Constant becomes rich through dumb luck, and his incredible wealth turns him into a monster. In *God Bless You, Mr. Rosewater*, it is difficult to decide whether the rich or poor characters are more pitiful, but in every case, their lives are controlled by money or the lack of it. Vonnegut points out that, left unchecked, capitalism will erode the democratic foundations of the United States. If families are allowed to accumulate enormous fortunes and pass them along generation after generation, they become a hereditary aristocracy, depriving other Americans of the opportunity to rise out of poverty. Vonnegut constantly encourages his readers to imagine how great this country could be if we only abided by basic principles of fairness and consideration for others.

Vonnegut also criticizes the capitalist system for encouraging people to think of themselves as individuals rather than as members of extended families. At the University of Chicago, Vonnegut studied under Dr. Robert Redfield, an anthropologist who advanced the theory that human beings evolved as members of folk societies composed of extended families. Now that these folk societies have fragmented under the pressure of industrialization, people are left with a longing for community that cannot be satisfied. Redfield's ideas meshed closely with Vonnegut's own experiences. As an adult he found himself yearning for the large extended family that had supported him during his youth in Indianapolis, and this desire for a meaningful community is found throughout his fiction. Most of Vonnegut's characters feel alienated from their families and strive to create artificial families. In *Player Piano*, the engineers call their boss's wife "Mom," and they reinforce their emotional bonds during a yearly retreat on a private island, where they act like overgrown boys. In *The Sirens of Titan*, Boaz finally finds a family among the harmoniums in the caves on Mercury. *Cat's Cradle* introduces two terms for different kinds of artificial families. A *karass* is a team organized by God to do His will, while a *granfalloon* is a meaningless association of people, such as a fraternal group or a nation. In *Slapstick*, Vonnegut imagines a future in which the U.S. government issues every citizen a new middle name in order to create artificial extended families and provide a sense of belonging to an increasingly alienated population. Although these artificial families provide some comfort to their members, they never fully succeed in replicating the sense of security found in true folk societies. Nevertheless, they are valuable because they give human beings a noble purpose for living. As Vonnegut put it in the epigraph for *Bluebeard*, quoting his son Mark: "We are here to help each other get through this thing, whatever it is."

This is probably Vonnegut's closest approach to an answer to a question posed in all of his novels: "What is the meaning of life?" *The Sirens of Titan* mocks those who would search for meaning in outer space by beginning with the statement that "Everyone now knows how to find the meaning of life within himself" (1). *Cat's Cradle* argues that all answers to the question are lies, and the best we can do is to live by the lies that make us "brave and kind and happy and healthy." In *Breakfast of Champions*, Kilgore Trout finds the question "What is the purpose of life?" written on a bathroom wall. Trout's answer, "To be the eyes and ears and conscience of the Creator of the Universe, you fool," sounds pretty good until we recall that Vonnegut is an atheist (67–68). Without a Creator to report back to, Trout's answer is inadequate. Vonnegut points this out by repeatedly referring to Trout as "the eyes and ears of the Creator of the Universe," even as he reports on prostitutes who have given up their freedom along with their will to live. As Trout chronicles one meaningless life after another, readers are left to wonder how a compassionate creator could stand by and do nothing while such reports come in. Of course, Trout is actually a medium for Vonnegut's messages to his readers about the sorry state of life in modern America. He is *our* eyes and ears, and his reports are meant to stir *our* consciences and encourage us to do something to help our fellow human beings. In Vonnegut's novels, to search for any greater meaning in life is dangerous folly.

Vonnegut's scientific training and his position in public relations at General Electric encouraged his abiding interest in the role of science and technology in American society. Although Vonnegut admires the curiosity and ingenuity of scientists, he condemns their failure to look up from their microscopes and consider the consequences of their discoveries. *Player Piano* takes the trend toward automation that Vonnegut observed at GE to its logical conclusion. All workers, aside from a few specialized engineers, have been replaced by machines, with devastating consequences for the self-esteem of the displaced workers. *God Bless You, Mr. Rosewater* also asks what can be done with people who have been made obsolete by machines. *Cat's Cradle* portrays the inventor of the atomic bomb as totally unconcerned about how his invention might be used. In *Deadeye Dick*, Vonnegut reacts to an even more horrifying weapon, the neutron bomb, which was designed to kill people while leaving buildings intact. Rudy Walz, the novel's protagonist, accidentally kills a pregnant woman by firing his father's gun out of an open window. The novel suggests that scientists who place nuclear weapons in the hands of politicians are just as irresponsible as the father who let a ten year old have access to a gun. In spite of all this, it would be inaccurate to classify Vonnegut as "anti-technology." He recognizes that human beings have an insatiable curiosity about the world around them, and he appreciates the joy that comes from scientific inquiry and discovery. In recent interviews and speeches, he acknowledges that today's scientists are deeply concerned about the social and cultural implications of their discoveries, and he hails this as an important step forward for humanity.

VONNEGUT'S CAREER

During the course of a fifty-year career, Vonnegut's reputation as a writer has had its ups and downs. In the 1950s, he published short stories in magazines that were intended to appeal to a wide audience, including the *Saturday Evening Post, Colliers, Esquire, Ladies Home Journal*, and *Cosmopolitan*. These magazines were known as "slicks" because of their glossy covers. The stories they published came to be known as "slick fiction," indicating not only where they were published but also that they were, in Vonnegut's words, "low-grade, simplistic, undisturbing sort of writing" (Allen 52), the literary equivalent of a television situation-comedy. Vonnegut soon learned what would please the editors and readers of these magazines, and for over ten years, he paid the bills by writing slick fiction. Many of these stories are collected in *Welcome to the Monkey House*. While they are entertaining and a pleasure to read, Vonnegut did not take them seriously, and they will not be discussed in detail in this book. Vonnegut's attitude toward his novels is quite different. He writes these with no hope for great monetary reward, but simply because he feels compelled to express himself. Before the incredible success of *Slaughterhouse-Five*, Vonnegut had little reason to expect that his novels would make him rich. In 1952, his first effort, *Player Piano*, was greeted by a favorable review in the *New York Times*, but it did not sell very well. When Bantam brought out the paperback version in 1954, they gave it a new title, *Utopia-14*, and a garish cover intended to make it appeal to science fiction fans. Although this probably boosted sales of the book, it hurt Vonnegut's reputation among critics, most of whom considered science fiction to be beneath their notice. Vonnegut's next two novels, *The Sirens of Titan* and *Mother Night*, were both published as paperback originals. Paperbacks are not usually reviewed, but they do sell better than hardcover books, so Vonnegut began to make a name for himself among average readers who pick up a novel in a drug store or a bus station to while away a few hours. The lack of critical attention hurt Vonnegut's pride, but he was gratified to begin receiving letters from people who had discovered his books and who hoped he would write more. The publishers also began to pay more attention to Vonnegut because his paperbacks were selling well. Although it was originally written for the paperback market, *Cat's Cradle* was issued in both hardcover and paperback in 1963 because of Vonnegut's proven ability to sell books. This established a pattern that would persist for the rest of his career. All of his subsequent novels were published in both formats, so they received the attention of critics and were also available to the general public. *Cat's Cradle* was praised by both professional critics and average readers, and Vonnegut began to reach a wider audience. His fame and critical reputation peaked with the publication of *Slaughterhouse-Five* in 1969. Vonnegut had accomplished a rare feat in American literature: He had written a book that appealed to millions of readers and won effusive praise from professional critics. Published at the height of the Vietnam War, *Slaughterhouse-Five* spoke powerfully to a generation exhausted and demoralized by the pointless brutality of modern warfare. On the strength of this book alone, Vonnegut won a place for himself in American literature and in the cultural history of the nation.

  Slaughterhouse-Five had taken him twenty years to write, and after completing it, Vonnegut was exhausted. He felt that his career as a writer might be over. He had done what he had to do in dealing with his wartime experiences in Dresden, and now he could look for other ways to spend his time, but the urge to write persisted. He struggled with his next novel, *Breakfast of Champions*, which was based on material that he had removed from *Slaughterhouse-Five*. When it was finally published in 1973, the novel was savagely attacked by critics, and even the most die-hard Vonnegut fans had to admit that it was a disappointment. Vonnegut's reputation continued to slide with the publication of *Slapstick* in 1976. Many readers began to suspect that Vonnegut's best work was behind him. Because *Breakfast of Champions* and *Slapstick* do not approach Vonnegut's usual standard, they will not be discussed further in this volume.

Vonnegut made a strong comeback with the publication of *Jailbird* in 1979. The novel is not only far superior to *Slapstick*, it also announces a new direction in Vonnegut's work. With the exception of *Galapagos* (1985) and *Timequake* (1997), Vonnegut's most recent works are realistic novels firmly based in American history. *Jailbird* weaves together the struggles of the labor movement and the Watergate scandal, corporate intrigue, and contemporary politics in a masterful story that demonstrates that Vonnegut still has plenty to say about America. *Jailbird* is clearly superior to *Deadeye Dick*, his other realistic novel of the period (1982). Although *Deadeye Dick* is a powerful indictment of politicians who play with weapons of mass destruction, Vonnegut dealt with this theme more effectively in *Cat's Cradle* and *Slaughterhouse-Five*, so *Deadeye Dick* will not be discussed in detail in subsequent chapters. *Bluebeard*, which contains Vonnegut's most profound thoughts on the role of the artist in modern society and his most convincing female characters, is the best of his late novels. *Bluebeard* is a virtuoso performance by a master craftsman, and a close reading of the novel provides an opportunity to assess Vonnegut's achievement as a novelist, so it has been chosen for extensive discussion in the final chapter of this study. *Galapagos* is something of an anomaly among Vonnegut's later works. It covers a time period of over a million years, and it is narrated by a ghost, but its real hero is evolution. Vonnegut clearly struggled with the challenges of telling such a story, and although the result is an interesting experiment, it lacks the human warmth that makes Vonnegut's best fiction memorable. The same could be said of Vonnegut's most recent novel, *Timequake* (1997), which brings back the beloved Kilgore Trout and contains many autobiographical fragments and philosophical musings. In the opening pages, Vonnegut confesses that the book is a collection of fragments from a novel that failed, and critics have been quick to point out that Vonnegut would have been better off abandoning the project. Along with *Hocus Pocus* (1990), a slightly better effort that nevertheless breaks no new ground, *Timequake* will not be discussed further in this volume.

After a career lasting more than fifty years, Vonnegut continues to write. All of his books are in print, and new readers discover him every day. His best works force them to take a hard look at contemporary social problems and make them laugh at the same time. Vonnegut's novels deal with the most profound issues of human existence in a style that is accessible to everyone. Although they demonstrate that there are plenty of reasons to be pessimistic about the future of the planet, they also point out reasons for hope. Vonnegut has said that artists should "serve society" by being "agents of change" and introducing new ideas (*Wampeters, Foma & Granfalloons* 237). According to these standards, Vonnegut has fulfilled his artistic mission by encouraging his readers to be both more skeptical and more compassionate.

Player Piano
(1952)

Player Piano was Kurt Vonnegut's first novel, and it earned many positive reviews. Several critics suggested that it announced the arrival of an important American novelist. In *Player Piano*, Vonnegut introduces many of the themes that are central to his later novels.

Player Piano is set in the future after a fictional third world war. During the war, while most Americans were fighting overseas, the nation's managers and engineers developed ingenious automated systems that allowed the factories to operate with only a few workers. The novel begins about ten years after the war, when most factory workers have been replaced by machines. Critics have often compared *Player Piano* with Aldous Huxley's *Brave New World* and George Orwell's *1984*. The three novels are categorized as "utopian" because they describe future worlds where all-powerful governments attempt to control every aspect of human life. Utopian novels take their name from Thomas More's *Utopia*, published in 1555, which described an ideal human society based on reason and logic. More recent utopian novels, such as those by Vonnegut, Orwell, and Huxley, describe how governments can use technology to control individuals, and all three authors predict a bleak future for humankind if current trends continue.

But upon closer inspection, *Player Piano* is not really about a distant, high-tech future. *Player Piano* is a satire on post-World War II America. Rather than focusing on amazing technological innovations, the novel describes the logical consequences of social forces already apparent in the 1950s. These forces include an uncritical faith in technology and "progress," an insatiable desire for material possessions, a lack of interest in politics, and a deliberate effort to encourage women to leave the work force.

Player Piano takes all of these social trends one step further and asks, What will America look like if we continue down the path of mechanization? The novel describes an almost fully mechanized society run by a small, elite corps of managers and engineers. The entire economy is managed by an enormous computer that determines how many television sets and toasters the nation needs. Computerized tests determine who gets into college and which of the college graduates may go on to earn the doctoral degree that is required for all but menial work. Even those with doctorates are at the mercy of machines that decide who is fit for what job based on their records and test scores. Those who are not chosen for the few positions available in the manager-engineer elite are given two options: the army or the "Reconstruction and Reclamation Corps" (20). Known as the "Reeks and Wrecks," these men who have been rejected by the system spend their days filling potholes and flushing storm drains. The sexist assumptions of the 1950s that tended to limit employment opportunities for women seem to have been written into law in *Player Piano*. Aside from a few female secretaries for top male executives, only men work outside the home.

In *Player Piano*, Vonnegut created a vision of the future that was intended to warn 1950s America about the perils of their worship of technological progress. Although some of the details, like computers running on vacuum tubes, seem dated to the contemporary reader, Vonnegut's indictment of our unquestioning faith in science and technology is more relevant than ever in the twenty-first century.

PLOT DEVELOPMENT

Player Piano develops two parallel plot lines that converge only briefly, at the beginning and the end of the novel. The most important plot line tells the story of Dr. Paul Proteus, an intelligent, thirty-five-year-old factory manager. The second plot line describes the American tour of the Shah of Bratpuhr, spiritual leader of six million residents of a distant, under-developed nation. Although the two plot lines are almost entirely independent of one another, they work together to paint a more complete picture of American society than either one could produce alone. Proteus lives and works within the system, but the Shah is a visitor from a very different culture. The parallel plot lines allow Vonnegut to show how the system looks from the inside and from the outside.

Paul Proteus is the ultimate insider. His father was the first "National, Industrial, Commercial, Communications, Foodstuffs, and Resources Director" (2). As his lengthy title suggests, Dr. George Proteus had almost complete control over the nation's economy and was more powerful than the President of the United States. As its first director, Paul's father is widely regarded as the father of the unified industrial system that was created during the Third World War. Paul is expected to follow in his father's footsteps, and as the novel opens, he seems ready to do just that. At the relatively young age of thirty-five, he is already in charge of an enormous, almost completely automated factory, the Ilium Works. But in spite of his good fortune, Paul is vaguely dissatisfied with the industrial system and his place in it. Throughout the novel, he considers alternatives, but the system is so large and complex that there are few opportunities to live outside of it. Paul considers buying one of the few farms that has not been absorbed by the agricultural industry, but he realizes that he lacks the skills to do anything but manage machines. He thinks about just quitting and living on the wealth that he has accumulated, but a life with no work seems even worse than his current dilemma. Paul feeds his fantasy life with novels about barrel-chested frontiersmen who survive by their strength and cunning and revel in the freedom of unspoiled nature.

A visit from an old friend, Ed Finnerty, shakes Paul out of his dream world. Finnerty has risen to the top of the system because of his brilliance, even though he refuses to play by the rules. He is a rebel looking for a cause, and he senses a rebellious streak in Paul that he hopes to develop. When he shows up at Paul's door, he has quit his important job in Washington, D.C., and he intends to live outside the system, just as Paul has dreamed of doing. Paul and Finnerty visit a bar in the "Homestead" section of town, where workers who have been displaced by machines live out their meaningless lives in shoddy, mass-produced houses. There they meet an Episcopal minister with an M.A. in anthropology named Lasher who puts into words the unfairness of the system that the two engineers have only vaguely sensed. Lasher tells them that his son, who did not pass the entrance exams for college, hanged himself rather than face a meaningless life in the army or the "Reeks and Wrecks." In fact, Lasher has no son, and he tells Paul the story as a kind of psychological experiment, but it still has a powerful effect on Paul. He realizes that by taking away their jobs, the system has robbed men of their dignity, and even of the will to live.

The story strengthens Paul's resolve to quit the system, but he is not bold enough to make a clean break as Finnerty has done. Finnerty is disappointed with Paul and takes up with Lasher, who is the leader of a rebel group known as the "Ghost Shirt Society." When Paul's superiors ask him to betray Finnerty and Lasher, he finally summons the courage to quit. Soon after, he is given a drugged drink and captured by the Ghost Shirt Society. They intend to use his famous name by making him the official leader of the organization. But Paul is a leader in name only. The Ghost Shirts keep him in a small, locked room for his own protection and allow him out only to appear at meetings.

One of these meetings is raided, and Paul is captured by the police. At his trial for treason, Paul responds to questions by reciting answers that have been carefully scripted by Lasher and Finnerty to serve as an indictment of the system. But the prosecutor forces Paul to abandon his script by asking him about his relationship with his famous father. Because he is wearing a lie detector, Paul is unable to deny that his hatred for the system is based on his hatred for his father, who was too busy running the country to attend to Paul when he was a boy.

The trial is cut short when the Ghost Shirts rise in rebellion and seize control of Ilium. The displaced workers smash the machines that took their jobs without stopping to consider which machines are useful, even critical, to human life. Paul and the other leaders of the Ghost Shirts retreat to his old office and view the destruction from afar. Other cities also rebel, but their rebellions are quickly put down, and Ilium is isolated. The next day an automated helicopter broadcasts a tape that demands that the people turn over their "false leaders," but most people are too busy repairing the machines they so recently smashed. As the city smolders and its residents enjoy their newly regained creativity, Paul and the other Ghost Shirt leaders turn themselves in to face certain execution as traitors.

The second plot line describes the Shah of Bratpuhr's visit to the United States. Both satirical and utopian novels often use visitors as a plot device because as the society is explained to the visitor, it is also being explained to the reader. A visitor who does not share the culture and values of the society provides a different perspective, which enables the satirist to point out the shortcomings of the system. For instance, when the Shah sees a crew from the Reeks and Wrecks working on the road, he calls them "Takaru," which means "slaves" (22–23). Although his guide struggles to convince him that the men are not slaves but "citizens," the Shah insists on calling them slaves, and his mistake makes an important point. Although they are still officially citizens of the

United States, the industrial system does not allow them to make any significant choices and has, in effect, reduced them to the status of slaves.

The Shah's tour of the United States also allows Vonnegut to describe aspects of life that escape the notice of Paul Proteus. The Shah visits the home of a statistically "average" American citizen, a typical university, a barbershop, and even Carlsbad Caverns, the home of EPICAC XIV, the supercomputer that runs the American economy. More importantly, the Shah's reactions provide ironic commentary on the American gospel of technology and progress. When he visits the home of the "average American," his guide proudly displays the "ultrasonic dishwasher and clotheswasher" that allow the housewife to complete her chores "in a matter of seconds" (164). The Shah is not impressed. He wants to know why she is in such a hurry to finish her work. What does she do then, he wonders. The only answer he can think of is that she has plenty of time to watch television. The Shah's perspective allows Vonnegut to highlight the banality of middle-class American life. Appliances save time, but people do not know what to do with the time they have. As the Shah leaves, he has one word of advice for the couple, *"Brahouna!"*—"Live!" (165).

The Shah begins and ends his trip in Ilium, which provides a physical connection to the main plot line. More important are the thematic connections between the two plot lines, and these will be discussed in the section on thematic issues.

CHARACTER DEVELOPMENT

Dr. Paul Proteus is the protagonist, or main character, of *Player Piano*. As the son of Dr. George Proteus, the first director of the national industrial system, Paul seems destined to rise high in the organization. He is intelligent and fortunate that his skills as an engineer and manager are just what the employment machines require. But as the novel opens, he is troubled by a vague sense of dissatisfaction with his job, his life, and the system in general. As he goes through the motions at work, he is "annoyed, bored, queasy" (7).

Paul's unusual name, "Proteus," may provide some clues to his character. In Greek mythology, Proteus is a sea monster that can change his shape at will. His battle with Odysseus is found in Homer's *Odyssey*. In a sense, Paul Proteus also lacks a definite shape. He has no true identity but changes to suit the circumstances. When he goes to Homestead, he takes an old, beat-up car and replaces his business suit with a leather jacket in a desperate attempt to blend in with his surroundings. However, unlike the original Proteus, Paul's changes are forced on him by circumstances beyond his control. He spends most of the novel looking for something to believe in and waiting for someone to give him orders so that he will not have to take responsibility for his actions. In his youth, the industrial system provided him with a ready-made set of beliefs and told him what to do, but he has lost faith in the system.

Paul's later involvement with the Ghost Shirt Society repeats the same pattern of unquestioning allegiance to a large organization. For Paul, the main appeal of the Ghost Shirts is that they force him to do what they want or be killed. Rather than resenting this loss of freedom, Paul finds it "liberating" because he no longer has to make his own decisions and take responsibility for his choices (297). After the revolution fails, Paul finally recognizes his motives for joining the Ghost Shirts. He was "eager to join a large, confident organization with seeming answers to the problems that had made him sorry to be alive" (334).

Not surprisingly, Paul does not have much insight into other people, even those who are closest to him. As he indulges his fantasy about living the life of a frontier farmer, he imagines that his status-conscious wife Anita will love the ramshackle farmhouse he intends to buy. Although she has decorated their home in colonial style, behind the antique facades she has stashed all of the modern conveniences. She may love the colonial look, but she is unwilling to abandon the modern world. Paul imagines that with his superior brainpower he can "subtly re-educate" Anita, as if this will be as simple as reprogramming a computer (135). But as the novel reminds readers again and again, human beings are more complex than machines. Paul's inability to recognize this dooms all of his plans to failure.

Paul gains some insights into his own motives during his trial near the end of the novel. Under cross-examination and connected to a lie detector, he is forced to admit that his hatred for the industrial system comes from an unacknowledged hatred for his cold, emotionally distant father. The prosecutor hopes to use this admission to discredit the whole rebel movement, but Paul points out that we are all "motivated by something pretty sordid" and this is an essential part of what makes us human (317). In this moment, Paul becomes a representative man of the machine age. His lack of a stable identity, his inability to understand himself or others, and his desire for a powerful organization that can answer his nagging questions are revealed to be symptomatic of the times, and not just personal failings. Through the characterization of Paul

Proteus, Vonnegut has shown the debilitating effects of living in a technological age that has lost touch with humane values.

Ed Finnerty is Paul's only friend, and like Paul, he has become disillusioned with the system. Unlike Paul, Finnerty is a man of many talents. Finnerty's intelligence and insight have taken him to the top of the organization, but when he visits Paul he has already quit, and he hopes to persuade Paul to do the same. Finnerty is a rebel, and he is never really at home in the conservative, tightly knit "family" of engineers and managers. In sharp contrast to his clean-cut colleagues, Finnerty often goes weeks without changing his suit or washing. He regularly brings prostitutes from Homestead to formal dinners attended by engineers and their wives. For years Paul dismissed Finnerty's behavior as merely eccentric, but eventually he realized that it was actually a carefully calculated insult to the whole system and everything it represents. The contrast between Proteus and Finnerty allows Vonnegut to explore how a very different sort of man behaves in a mechanized world.

As the son of "poor and stupid parents," Finnerty is an outsider in a world where talent for engineering is often regarded as hereditary (35). But as a highly intelligent member of the engineering elite, he is also an outsider in the world of his parents. Finnerty's only joy in life comes from his bursts of creative energy, when the rest of the world falls away, and he is completely absorbed by the problem to be solved. For most of his life, Finnerty did not take the time to consider the social consequences of his creativity.

When he finally does take a hard look at the nightmare he has helped to create, he devotes himself with equal energy to destroying it. When the destruction of the Ilium Works is complete, Finnerty sums up his thoughts on the motives behind such upheavals in human history. "Things don't stay the way they are. . . . It's too entertaining to try to change them" (332). Finnerty embodies this amoral desire for change for its own sake that the novel reveals as an important motive for human actions.

Paul's wife Anita and his nemesis Lawson Shepherd may be considered together, since they share an overdeveloped sense of competitiveness that eventually brings them together as a couple. Anita is a beautiful, ambitious woman who must channel her ambition into promoting her husband's career because the system does not allow women to pursue their own careers. She is frustrated by Paul's lack of drive, and she constantly encourages him to seek higher positions. She goes so far as to write scripts for Paul's meetings with top executives, hoping that if he says the right things he will advance within the organization. She thinks of the system as a battleground where Paul must slaughter his rivals in order to advance.

Lawson Shepherd is also fiercely competitive. He pursues his advancement by constantly attempting to make his rivals look bad. Most of his fellow engineers regard him with amused contempt, but his character demonstrates another response to the industrial system. Since the system is based on a rigid hierarchy, in which pay, prestige, and responsibilities increase as one reaches higher levels, there is some logic in regarding it as a ladder that one must climb over the backs of defeated rivals. The system may reward this attitude, but the characters of Anita and Shepherd show that it results in a twisted, deformed personality.

The other minor characters achieve significance by highlighting one of the novel's major themes, so they will be dealt with in the following section on thematic issues.

THEMATIC ISSUES

The central themes of *Player Piano* are all related to one basic question: What is the human cost of technological progress? Describing a world where machines have taken over most jobs allows Vonnegut to explore this question on many levels. He reveals the motives behind the constant desire for more and better machines. He acknowledges that machines contribute to human happiness, even as he calls our attention to the negative consequences of mechanization that are often overlooked. *Player Piano* points out that basic human values such as integrity and dignity will be challenged as the level of mechanization increases. Even the nuclear family may be torn apart by the social forces created by technological progress.

Player Piano shows that the primary motive for technological progress is the "restless, erratic insight and imagination of the gadgeteer" that has been considered "peculiarly American" ever since the nation's founding (4–5). Bud Calhoun, an engineer at the Ilium Works, is a perfect example of this love of invention for its own sake. He has modified his car so that it responds to voice commands and engineered the seats so that they recline at the touch of a button. But his love of gadgets and his skill at designing them leads to his downfall. He designs a machine that performs his job better than he can, so he is laid off. The irony is obvious, and it points to one of the novel's central themes. The inventiveness that provides so many Americans with their principal joy in life may eventually make them obsolete.

Bud's story also illustrates the shortsightedness of many engineers. He is so engrossed by the problem of designing a machine to replace himself that he never thinks about what will happen if he succeeds. If engineers do not stop to think about the personal consequences of their inventions, how can we expect them to consider the social consequences? The novel suggests that we cannot expect engineers to do this, but that someone must think ahead about what sort of technological progress will really improve the human condition. The leaders of the Ghost Shirt Society plan to decide which machines to destroy and which to save after the revolution, but their followers destroy every machine they can get their hands on. When the destruction is complete, they begin to rebuild them with a similar lack of regard for the consequences. Amid the ashes of the old system, Paul finds Bud and several other men happily repairing a soft-drink machine, "eager to recreate the same old nightmare" (340). Although Paul looks ahead to consider the consequences of their creativity, Bud and his friends are too engrossed in the joy of tinkering to think about the human consequences of what they create. As the Ghost Shirts planned the revolution, Bud was just as happy designing weapons as he had been tinkering with his car. Finnerty expresses the dangerous attitude of some engineers at the end of the novel, "If only it weren't for the people ... always getting tangled up in the machinery, ... earth would be an engineer's paradise" (332). This quote clearly shows how some engineers lose sight of the fact that their machines should serve people and make their lives easier. In the future described in *Player Piano*, people have been made to serve machines with disastrous consequences.

In spite of the novel's clear warning about what will happen if machines become more important than the people they are meant to serve, it would be an oversimplification to say that the novel has an "anti-machine" theme. In addition to the joy that comes from creating machines, *Player Piano* depicts the satisfaction that comes from watching them in action. When Paul is plagued by doubts about the system, he retreats to the assembly line to listen to the "exciting music" of the machines (11). Paul almost becomes hypnotized by the dance-like movements of a machine that wraps insulation around a cable. His reservations about the industrial system are put aside as he contemplates the "entertaining and delightful" machines (9). As a result of highly productive machines, the average American has a house full of useful, cleverly designed gadgets. No one goes hungry, and because of the nation's

unquestionable industrial superiority, there are no more wars. In strictly
material terms, human life has never been better.

However, all of this prosperity comes at a great human cost. Ironically,
as machines take on more human characteristics—as they dance, make
music, and do useful work—human beings find fewer and fewer outlets
for their creativity. The employment machines that match people with
suitable occupations recognize only machine-like qualities in people, and
this has disastrous results for those who do not excel at the officially
approved vocations of manager or engineer. Even Bud Calhoun, who
has proven ability as a designer, is rejected for design work by a machine
that regards his grades and test scores as too low. Artists fare even
worse. Paul comforts his wife Anita by praising her artistic ability and
pointing out that it is a "tragedy" that none of the machines can recognize it. But this criticism of the system overlooks a more basic problem.
Although the issue is never discussed directly, women are evidently not
allowed to work outside the home, regardless of their abilities. Sexism
is built into the system, and opportunities for women are even more
severely restricted than they are for men.

If a machine fails to recognize a man's abilities, then his only options
are the army and the "Reeks and Wrecks." Neither of these occupations
offer any possibility for creativity or a sense of satisfaction with a job
well done. The novel depicts the "Reeks and Wrecks" only in passing,
but every glimpse confirms the corrosive effects of a lack of meaningful
work on the men's self-esteem. They behave more like boys than like
men, opening hydrants and sailing paper boats, throwing rocks at squir-
rels. When they are given orders by a member of the "elite," they show
their scorn for a system that has robbed them of their manhood and their
sense of purpose. The name they have given themselves, the "Reeks and
Wrecks," expresses their sense of themselves as broken men (wrecks)
whose lot in life stinks (reeks).

Although the loss of human dignity that follows mechanization is
more obvious among the "Reeks and Wrecks," it also plagues the engineering elite. Paul has an important job that gives him high prestige, but
he spends most of his time at work reading adventure novels. When he
does have to work, he merely responds to one of the warning lights that
tells him something is wrong in the Works. He does not decide how
many refrigerators the Works should produce. All important decisions
are made by the supercomputer that runs the economy. At thirty five,
Paul realizes that his best work is already behind him. He longs for the
days when he and the other engineers set up the machines that now run
themselves. That important work gave Paul a sense of direction and

purpose that he now lacks. Paul describes himself as a "derelict," a ship adrift, without a "hand on the tiller" (306).

Paul's lack of direction in middle age leads to an obsession with integrity that develops into one of the novel's major thematic issues. Paul feels that he lacks integrity, and his thoughts on the subject show that he is not really clear on what integrity is. The issue becomes important when Paul is asked to betray his friend Finnerty to demonstrate his loyalty to the system. He considers this "about as basic as an attack on integrity could be" (135). So loyalty to friends is essential to integrity, but more is involved. Finnerty tries to get Paul to add to his definition of integrity by telling him a story about Henry Thoreau and Ralph Waldo Emerson, two nineteenth-century American writers. In 1846, Thoreau was in jail for failing to pay a tax as a way of protesting the Mexican War. His friend Emerson came to visit him and asked, "Henry, why are you here?" Thoreau's famous reply was "Ralph, why aren't you here?" Paul misses the point of the story, so Finnerty sums it up for him. "You shouldn't let fear of jail keep you from doing what you believe in" (143). But for Paul, fear of jail is not the real problem. Instead, "the big trouble . . . was finding something to believe in" (143). As the novel defines it, integrity means having a definite set of beliefs that you are willing to defend, regardless of the consequences. Paul lacks integrity because he does not believe in anything except a vague notion of personal loyalty.

An anonymous prostitute, picked up on the street by the Shah of Bratpur, tells a story that contributes to the novel's definition of integrity. She explains that she is on the street, trying to earn money in one of the few ways that are still open to women, because her husband is a fiction writer whose first book was rejected for having an "anti-machine theme" (244). As the Shah's State Department escort, Dr. Halyard, points out, he is lucky not to be in jail for violating the anti-sabotage laws. The woman explains that he wrote the book because "he had to write it," and he did not care about the consequences. To Dr. Halyard, the writer's artistic integrity is a clear sign that the man is "maladjusted" and in need of psychiatric help. But his wife explains that he is determined to raise the big questions about human life, "where people are, where they're going, and why they're going there" (245). Of course, these are the same questions that *Player Piano* raises, and they come up again and again in Vonnegut's fiction.

The industrial system depicted in *Player Piano* may be described as paternalistic because it provides for all of its citizens' needs and makes all of their major decisions for them. The term "paternalism" derives from the Latin word for father (*pater*), and the system in *Player Piano* acts like an all-powerful father. The human cost of living in a paternalistic system is one of the novel's major themes. The system takes over the role traditionally played by fathers in nuclear families and reduces all people, regardless of age, to the status of children. During the Shah's visit to a typical American family, we are told that average citizens are given a small weekly allowance, but they are not permitted to decide on major purchases. The central computer makes these big, "grown-up" decisions for them.

We have already seen how the "Reeks and Wrecks" behave like boys, but the paternalistic system also turns the engineering elite into overgrown children. Paul takes "childish" delight in his adventure novels (137). For two weeks every year, the system's top executives act like overgrown boys at a summer camp called "The Meadows," where every minute of the day is planned in advance. The men are ordered from one activity to the next by the insistent commands of the loudspeaker system. They are divided into teams and encouraged to compete with one another as a way of building team spirit. The entertainment consists of a play that oversimplifies human life and reinforces the idea that the industrial system is an all-good, all-powerful father for everyone.

Player Piano suggests that the ever-increasing mechanization of the modern world may result in a system that will end hunger and war, but at what cost? The novel's answer is that for every advance in efficiency and prosperity people must pay with a loss of personal responsibility, freedom, integrity, and dignity. The clearest statements of this theme come during Paul's trial for treason. In order to test the lie detector, the judge asks Paul to tell what he considers to be a lie. Paul responds, "Every new piece of scientific knowledge is a good thing for humanity" (315). When asked to tell the truth, he says, "The main business of humanity is to do a good job of being human beings, . . . not to serve as appendages to machines, institutions and systems" (315). These two statements sum up the basic message of *Player Piano*, and they resonate through all of Vonnegut's later fiction.

SYMBOLISM

Several symbols contribute to the development of *Player Piano*'s central theme. The novel's title comes from one of the first machines to replace a human being. The Homestead bar where Paul and Finnerty become involved with the Ghost Shirt Society has a player piano, and a close examination of how a player piano works and how it is described in the novel will reveal its symbolic importance.

Player pianos were among the first devices for recording sound. The recording is made by a musician playing a tune on a special piano that punches holes in a revolving roll of paper every time the piano player hits a key. When the roll of perforated paper is put in a player piano, it makes the same keys go down in the same order and reproduces the original tune. The piano rolls resemble the perforated cards that contain all the essential information about the citizens of Ilium. Although player pianos were considered remarkable, even miraculous, at the turn of the century, they do not sound very good to modern ears because they cannot reproduce the subtle modulations of sound that make the performance of a gifted pianist so rewarding. The tunes are recognizable, all the notes are correct, but something important is missing. It is that human element, the emotional heart of the song, that player pianos cannot reproduce. In a similar way, the perforated computer cards cannot adequately represent the people they supposedly describe.

During Paul's first visit to the bar, Rudy Hertz, the machinist whose movements Paul recorded to create the master tape for the first automatic lathe, pops a nickel in the player piano to play a tune in Paul's honor. The player piano then reproduces the movements of a long forgotten pianist, just as the lathe in the Works reproduces Rudy's work. As the piano plays, the keys go down as if pressed by an invisible hand. Rudy points this out to Paul. "You can almost see a ghost sitting there playing his heart out" (31). Of course, the machine has no heart, and mechanization has made ghosts of men who once had jobs and a sense of purpose in life. Their contributions to the industrial system are invisible, like the hands that play the piano.

Player pianos are more versatile than other recording devices because they can also be played by a musician, just like a regular piano. After meeting Lasher at the bar and discussing the human problems caused by the industrial system, Finnerty sits down at the piano and begins "to lash at the keys . . . savagely improvising on the brassy, dissonant antique" (105). Finnerty's fury at the keyboard reflects his anger with a system that has ruined the lives of so many people. Dissonance is the opposite of harmony, and dissonant music is hard to listen to for long. The player piano, a symbol of the system, is described as "dissonant" because it destroys the harmony of human life, replacing it with the unpleasant noise of machines. Demonstrating his creativity, Finnerty improvises, making up the tune as he goes along, something no machine can do. His playing is described as "lash[ing]" the keyboard, reminding us of his new friend Lasher, who also wants to strike out against the system. Finnerty plays the piano; he does not allow the system that it represents to play him. His savage improvisation suggests that it is not too late for people to reclaim control of their lives.

A violent encounter between a cat and an automatic sweeping machine at the Works symbolizes the fate of living creatures in a thoroughly mechanized world. As the sweeper gets closer, Paul searches in vain for the switch that will turn it off, and the cat makes a last, desperate stand. Of course, the machine does not stop. It sucks up the cat and throws her into its "galvanized tin belly" (13). The sweeping machine is an obvious symbol for the system as a whole. The fact that Paul cannot find the switch that will stop it suggests that the system is out of control and will not even respond to the top executives who supposedly manage it. The cat may represent the workers who are now as disposable as the waste that the sweeper is designed to eliminate.

When the sweeper reaches the end of the aisle, it spits the cat, still alive, down a chute and into a freight car outside the building. The cat escapes from the car and climbs the fence that surrounds the works. As it reaches the electrified wire at the top, it explodes and falls, "dead and smoking, but outside" (13). This description of its death suggests a more specific symbolic significance for the cat. Like Paul and the other members of the Ghost Shirt Society, she makes a stand against the system. Although it is emotionally satisfying to stand up against a more powerful opponent, such defiance almost always ends in defeat. The system sucks Paul up into its "tin belly" (the jail), and even though he escapes for a moment during the rebellion, he can no more escape the system than the cat can get out of the Works alive. At the end of the novel, he turns himself into the authorities to face certain execution for treason.

The cat's symbolic battle with the system resembles the doomed rebellion of the "Ghost Shirt Society," whose name was borrowed from a group of Native Americans who made a last-ditch stand against the white men in the 1890s. Although their revolt failed, by fighting and dying for their beliefs they became symbols of those beliefs, and they left a lasting record of resistance for future generations to admire and emulate. Lasher's rebellion is meant to prove that being a good human is more important than serving machines. In his mind at least, its primary value has always been symbolic. "He had created the revolution as a symbol, and was now welcoming the opportunity to die as one" (340).

A CULTURAL POETICS READING

Developed in the 1970s and 1980s, cultural poetics is a critical approach that attempts to read texts in their historical and cultural contexts. Cultural poetics critics define the term "text" quite broadly. In addition to works of literature, they examine histories, political speeches, letters, diaries, even advertisements and graffiti. One of the basic assumptions of cultural poetics is that, in order to understand a text, we must have some understanding of the time period and the culture in which the text was produced. Critics who adopt a cultural poetics approach see culture as an ongoing conversation between texts. Meaning is created by the way that texts talk to one another.

In order to arrive at a reading of a text, a cultural poetics critic attempts to answer three basic questions: How are the author's experiences and beliefs reflected in the text? What are the rules and expectations of the culture in which the text was produced? How does the text add to the ongoing conversation about those rules? This cultural poetics reading of Kurt Vonnegut's *Player Piano* will attempt to answer these three questions.

Vonnegut's experiences and beliefs are certainly represented in *Player Piano*. The Ilium Works is based on the General Electric plant in Schenectady, New York, where Vonnegut worked as a public relations man from 1947 to 1951, while he was writing *Player Piano*. During this time, he became fascinated by the scientific advances that were being made at GE's lab. He admired the genius of the researchers even as he became worried about their apparent lack of concern about how their discoveries would be used. These mixed feelings about scientists and engineers are clearly reflected in *Player Piano*. In the novel, these men derive their greatest joys from their research, but they rarely devote much thought to the human consequences of their discoveries.

In 1980, a Swedish newspaper asked Vonnegut for an essay on the topic "When I Lost My Innocence." Vonnegut's reply reveals how his attitude toward technological progress was shaped by his boyhood experiences working in the family hardware store. "An enthusiasm for technological cures for almost all forms of human discontent was the only religion of my family during the Great Depression" (*Palm Sunday* 62). But Vonnegut's faith in the "cunning devices and compounds on sale" in the family hardware store was shattered by the atomic bomb dropped on Hiroshima in 1945. "[T]he bombing of Hiroshima compelled me to see that a trust in technology, like all the other great religions of the world, had to do with the human soul" (63). Vonnegut sees the bombing of Hiroshima as a clear sign of the sickness of the collective soul of all industrialized nations. He traces the sickness to the fact that so many people consider death preferable to living "lives in the service of machines." In *Player Piano*, Paul Proteus's loss of faith in the religion of technology is not as sudden or dramatic as the change of heart that Vonnegut experienced, but it is just as profound. The novel challenges readers to contemplate the spiritual cost of technological progress, just as Hiroshima forced Vonnegut to question his faith in technology.

Vonnegut's experiences in public relations also come into play in the novel. In a brief but significant scene, the Shah of Bratpuhr picks up a woman whose husband is a struggling writer. She tells him that when he refused to write the kind of fiction that the system demands, he was told to report for work in public relations. The organization's *Manual* defines public relations as, "that profession specializing in the cultivation, by applied psychology in mass communication media, of favorable public opinion with regard to controversial issues and institutions" (242). In other words, public relations is the art of making people believe what the system wants them to believe. Vonnegut's job at GE was to observe the work in progress at the lab and find ways to get favorable stories about it into major magazines. While he was working there, the company's slogan, devised by one of his colleagues in public relations, was "At General Electric, Progress Is Our Most Important Product" (Klinkowitz, *Vonnegut in America* 16). It must have been difficult for someone whose faith in progress had so recently been shattered to write relentlessly positive prose about whatever innovations were coming out of the lab. Like the nameless writer in *Player Piano*, Vonnegut prefers to raise the big, troubling questions about human life, rather than pretend that all is well and try to make others believe it.

As we have seen, Vonnegut's experiences and beliefs are clearly reflected in *Player Piano*, but what were the rules and expectations of American culture in the 1940s and 1950s, and how does the novel add to the conversation about those rules? By the time Vonnegut was writing *Player Piano*, Franklin Roosevelt's New Deal and its Social Security system had convinced most Americans that they could look to the federal government to provide them with assistance when they needed it. In *Player Piano*, Vonnegut takes the idea of social security to its logical conclusion. All those who can work are guaranteed a job, and those who cannot are given pensions. All citizens have complete medical and dental coverage. But Vonnegut adds to the nation's conversation about the proper role of government by pointing out that all of this security comes at a high price in personal freedom.

After World War II, the American dream was a house in the suburbs with a television, washing machine, and a car in the garage. Because few houses were built in the 1930s during the Depression, or in the early 1940s because of the war, there was an acute housing shortage in the late 1940s. Bill Levitt responded to the demand by mass-producing identical houses on a large tract of land on Long Island that came to be known as "Levittown." Levitt's first houses even came with a television and a washing machine (Halberstam 135). Soon his approach to building houses was copied everywhere, and the modern suburb was born. In *Player Piano*, Vonnegut satirizes this standardized version of the American dream during the Shah's visit to the "typical" American family, the Hagstrohms. They live in a suburb of Chicago that consists of "three thousand dream houses for three thousand families with presumably identical dreams" (160). The Hagstrohms are the most carefully drawn minor characters in the novel, and the care that Vonnegut has taken to make them distinct individuals seems designed to point out the inadequacy of mass-produced housing. Vonnegut's father and grandfather were both architects, and they designed houses to suit the needs of particular families. Like Levittown, Vonnegut's fictional suburb is a model of efficiency and careful planning, but it has no soul.

During World War II, eight million women joined the work force, and the importance of their contribution to the war effort was recognized in national magazines and newspapers. Within two months of the end of the war, 800,000 women were fired from jobs in the aircraft industry, and within two years, over two million women had lost their jobs (Halberstam 588–89). The prevailing attitude at the time was that jobs should go to men returning from the war and that women should get married and stay at home to raise their families. The same magazines and newspapers that had encouraged women to take factory jobs during the war now claimed that it was "unfeminine" for a married woman to work outside the home. Women were told that they must not compete with men. Instead, they should devote their lives to caring for their husband and children. The magazines' advertisers portrayed women as satisfied owners of all the new labor-saving gadgets that were being produced after the war. Once again, *Player Piano* takes a distinct social trend and follows it to its logical conclusion. In the novel, the only women who work are single, and they are secretaries to prominent male managers. At first glance, the novel does not seem to question the notion that, as the old saying goes, "a woman's place is in the home." The issue is never raised directly. However, in the character of Anita, Paul Proteus's ambitious wife, we can see the consequences of being confined within such narrow limits. In many ways, Anita is better suited to the competitive world of corporate management than her laid-back husband, but because her culture prohibits her from competing with men, her ambition becomes obsessive, almost a form of mental illness. Deprived of the opportunity to use her skills, she becomes a one-dimensional caricature of a human being.

Player Piano is clearly a product of its times, as those times were refracted through the prism of Kurt Vonnegut's experiences and beliefs. As such it provides insights into American culture during the late 1940s and 1950s, and it introduces us to the central concerns of all of Vonnegut's later fiction.

The Sirens of Titan
(1959)

The Sirens of Titan, Kurt Vonnegut's second novel, is the easiest one to classify as science fiction (for a discussion of the conventions of science fiction, see chapter 2 of this volume). Unlike *Slaughterhouse-Five*, which mixes science fiction with scenes of brutal realism, *The Sirens of Titan* uses the techniques of science fiction from beginning to end. Since many literary critics consider science fiction to be beneath their notice, they have dismissed this novel as a "space opera," full of improbable action and adventure but lacking serious content. However a closer reading reveals that Vonnegut is actually poking fun at the conventions of the "space opera" at a time when this type of science fiction was moving from the pulp magazines to the movies and television and enjoying unprecedented popularity. Vonnegut is more interested in exploring the inner space of the human soul than in charting the unknown reaches of outer space. Vonnegut employs the conventions of science fiction, not for their own sake, but for the power they give him to explore the meaning and value of human life in a technological age.

The opening sentence of *The Sirens of Titan* should make it clear that this is not a typical science fiction novel: "Everyone now knows how to find the meaning of life within himself" (1). Science fiction usually takes the reader into the future, and so does *The Sirens of Titan*, but in this novel, the future is seen from an even more distant point in the future. Therefore, the narrator is looking backward to a time he calls the "Nightmare Ages," when people searched for the meaning of life outside themselves. In those days, beginning with the end of the Second World War, space exploration became the final quest for meaning in an apparently senseless universe. But in space, the explorers found just what they had found on earth, "a nightmare of meaninglessness without end" (1–2). By adopting the perspective of a wise observer looking back on the follies of earlier times, Vonnegut is telling us to read the novel as a satire of our own tendency to look for answers outside ourselves (for a discussion of satire, see chapter 2 of this volume). Rather than reveling in the wonders of space exploration, as most science fiction does, Vonnegut warns readers at the outset that it leads to just three things: "empty heroics, low comedy, and pointless death" (2). The rest of the novel delivers all three in abundance, so the reader must keep this warning in mind to avoid missing the true meaning hidden behind the space adventure.

PLOT DEVELOPMENT

A brief summary of the plot of *The Sirens of Titan* would convince someone who has never read the novel that it is the crudest form of science fiction. The novel consists of a series of improbable incidents connected by even less probable coincidences. The supposedly scientific explanations of strange phenomenon make little sense and often seem to contradict one another. However, if readers keep in mind that all this madness is meant to prove that the search for meaning outside of oneself is hopeless, the novel becomes an entertaining satire on the many methods humans have devised to put off that internal quest.

The story begins with a crowd waiting outside the Newport, Rhode Island, estate of Winston Niles Rumfoord. Rumfoord and his dog Kazak are scheduled to "materialize" briefly before once again disappearing for fifty-nine days. Rumfoord exists as a spiral of electricity orbiting the sun because he sailed his personal spaceship through a "chrono-synclastic infundibulum," a funnel in space and time (7–8). As a result, Rumfoord exists simultaneously at all points in his orbit and at all times of his existence. He can see the past and the future, and he can read minds. He materializes on earth every time our planet's orbit intersects his own.

Usually, Rumfoord allows only his wife and his butler to view his materializations, but this time he has summoned Malachi Constant, the richest man in America, because he wants to tell him about his future. Rumfoord tells Constant that he will travel to Mars where he will be "bred" with Rumfoord's wife Beatrice (21). He will then go to Mercury and return briefly to Earth before heading to his final destination, Titan, one of the moons of Saturn. Of course this all sounds incredible to Malachi Constant, but he does own a company that controls the last remaining spaceship capable of such a voyage. He promptly sells the company in an attempt to avoid the fate that Rumfoord has promised him. But of course he cannot avoid his fate, and he does eventually follow the itinerary laid out by Rumfoord.

At this point the story line doubles back to explain how Malachi Constant came to be such a wealthy man. It is purely a matter of "dumb luck" (67). His father discovered a system for picking stocks by matching their initials with the letters of the opening words of the Bible. He never revealed his secret to anyone but Malachi, and his son carried on his method after his death. Constant is known as the luckiest man on earth, and on the few occasions when he ponders his good fortune, his only conclusion is "somebody up there likes me" (15). But Constant's good luck runs out shortly after he meets Rumfoord. A worldwide depression wipes out his stock portfolio, lawsuits bankrupt his cigarette company, and in a drunken stupor, he gives away all of his oil wells. When two Martians arrive to recruit him for their army, he is ready to go.

At this point, the plot line skips ahead a few years. Constant, now known as "Unk," is a grizzled veteran of a Martian army that is made up of earthlings who have been kidnapped by Rumfoord to serve his secret purposes. Like all recruits, he has had his memory cleaned out, and a radio receiver implanted in his brain gives him orders that are enforced by jolts of pain. The radio tells him to strangle a man who is chained to a post in the middle of an immense reviewing ground. In front of the entire army, Unk carries out the order. Only many years later does he learn that the man he has killed is Stony Stevenson, his best friend. As the man dies, he tells Unk to look under a rock near Barracks 12 for a letter that will help him fill in the gaps in his memory. At this point Unk does not realize it, but he wrote the letter himself so that he would not forget important facts about his past. From the letter, Unk learns that the army of Mars will soon attack the earth. He also learns that he has a "mate" named Bee and a boy named Chrono and that is why he so stubbornly resists all efforts to clean out his memory. The letter instructs him to find Bee and Chrono, steal a spaceship, and escape. Unk tries, but he is caught by guards and brought before the real commander of the army, Winston Niles Rumfoord. Rumfoord informs Unk that his "mate" is actually Rumfoord's wife Beatrice and that Unk raped her aboard the spaceship that brought them both to Mars. Rumfoord does not tell Unk that he is really Malachi Constant, or that he is planning to use him as part of a spectacle that he will stage to establish a new religion on earth; however, the narrator does inform the reader of this plan.

Unk boards a spaceship with his "buddy" Boaz, thinking that they will overtake the other Martian ships that are beginning their invasion of earth, but once again, Rumfoord has other plans. He sets the ship's automatic navigation system to take it to Mercury. Boaz and Unk find themselves in deep caves below the surface of the planet, surrounded by strange kite-shaped creatures called "harmoniums" (188). The harmoniums live on the vibrations given off by Mercury's rotation around the sun, and Boaz develops a real affection for the creatures. He discovers that he can "feed" them with music from a record player on the spaceship. Unk spends his time looking for a way out of the caves, but Boaz is content with the love he feels for the harmoniums. Periodically, the harmoniums arrange themselves on the walls to spell out a message for Unk and Boaz. The messages, which actually come from Rumfoord, challenge them to think hard about how they can escape from the deep hole they find themselves in. After two years the answer is revealed. Unk turns the spaceship over and uses its sophisticated landing system to find a way out of the labyrinth of the cave. Boaz chooses to remain behind with his beloved harmoniums.

Unk's ship lands at a small church on Cape Cod where the Reverend C. Horner Redwine is waiting for him. During the two years Unk spent on Mercury, Rumfoord has created a new religion, "The Church of God the Utterly Indifferent" (219). He has prophesied that a weary veteran of the army of Mars will someday land at this church and assume his place as an important figure in the new religion. The invasion of the earth by Mars was a complete failure, but that is just what Rumfoord planned. He used the invasion as a way to convince all humans that they are brothers. Then he used their slaughter of the Martians as a way of making them feel guilty. Then he convinced people that God is completely indifferent to their success or failure in life. He used Malachi Constant as an example of the mistaken notion that luck is a sign of God's favor. Small figures representing Constant and known as "Malachis" are hung in effigy everywhere the faithful congregate. When Unk lands, he says just what the prophecy predicted that the "Space Wanderer" would say, and he is whisked off to Newport where Rumfoord is about to materialize (221). By now, Rumfoord's materializations have taken on all the trappings of a carnival. Crowds jam the grounds of Rumfoord's mansion, while he struts on an elevated stage that gives him easy access to every corner of the estate. Bee and Chrono, along with some of the few surviving members of the army of Mars, sell Malachis and other trinkets of the new religion outside the walls of the mansion. In a dramatic moment, intended to solidify the new religion's hold on the imaginations of the people, Rumfoord reveals that the Space Wanderer is actually Malachi Constant. Then he reunites Constant, Bee, and Chrono and sends them off to Titan, a moon of Saturn on a rocket he has already prepared.

When the three land on Titan, they discover that it is the one place in the universe where Rumfoord is constantly materialized, and so it has become his home. Rumfoord shares the moon with Salo from Tralfamadore, a distant planet inhabited entirely by machines. Salo is a messenger, sent eons earlier to deliver a message to the farthest reaches of the galaxy. His ship broke down on Titan, and he is waiting for a spare part. Traveling at the speed of light, his distress signal took 150,000 years to reach his home planet, but on Tralfamadore they have a powerful way to get things done. They have mastered the "Universal Will to Become," or U.W.T.B., and with it they can affect the thoughts and actions of human beings over immense distances. The novel tells us that Stonehenge, the Great Wall of China, and Nero's palace in Rome were all built as messages to Salo, telling him to be patient, that help was on the way. In fact, all of human history has been manipulated by the Tralfamadorians to serve their purposes. As a storm on the sun prepares to hurl him out of the solar system forever, Rumfoord, the novel's great manipulator, realizes that he has been manipulated by the Tralfamadorians in order to bring a spare part so Salo can repair his ship.

As the years go by on Titan, Malachi Constant lives the simple life of a farmer. Bee retreats to Rumfoord's mansion to write a refutation of her former husband's philosophy of an indifferent universe, and Chrono becomes the leader of the giant bluebirds of Titan. Although the three of them never become a loving family, they see each other from time to time and take care of each other as best they can. After Bee's death, Constant convinces Salo to take him back to earth, to Indianapolis, a city he has never visited, where he knows no one. Waiting to catch a bus to the city's center, Malachi Constant freezes to death in the snow.

CHARACTER DEVELOPMENT

The Sirens of Titan has two major characters, Malachi Constant and Winston Niles Rumfoord. Only two other characters are sufficiently well developed to merit consideration in this section: Beatrice Rumfoord and Boaz, Malachi Constant's companion on Mercury. Winston Niles Rumfoord is described as an American aristocrat. His family has been wealthy for many generations, and he grew up in an immense mansion in Newport, Rhode Island, where the coastline is dominated by mansions built for the wealthy in the late 1800s. As a child, Rumfoord had a keen interest in biology, and he amassed an impressive collection of shells and skeletons. The collection is housed in a small room of the mansion that Rumfoord chooses as the location for his first meeting with Malachi Constant, suggesting that the collection is still important to Rumfoord as a grown man. Described as a "museum of mortal remains," the collection consists of the remnants of "souls long gone" (19). This apparently insignificant detail provides an important clue to Rumfoord's character. It suggests that Rumfoord is unable to appreciate the importance of the human soul. As a grown man, he plays with people in the same careless way that he once played with shells. The army he creates on Mars consists of the hollowed out shells of men, deprived of their memories, wills, and identities. Rumfoord shows no remorse when he sends tens of thousands of them to their deaths.

In spite of this horrible flaw, Rumfoord is one of the most charming characters in Vonnegut's fiction. Everything he does he does with style. He has the courage to fly his personal spaceship into a chrono-synclastic infundibulum and the style to deal with the consequences as if they were only a minor inconvenience. Rumfoord exists as a wave phenomenon, rather than a physical body, and our first glimpse of him comes during one of his materializations, when he is temporarily visible on earth. In spite of this, what impresses Malachi Constant is not his unusual condition, but the natural attributes of a man of his class. Rumfoord is smug and has a strong sense of his superiority over others, and he manages to convince everyone else that he really is superior. How Rumfoord does this is something of a mystery. The novel often refers to his "almost singing" voice and its magical power to make others do what he wants, but Rumfoord's imposing physical appearance and his mannerisms also exude a sense of superiority (15). Keeping in mind the novel's fundamental distinction between the inwardness of the human soul and the outwardness of physical appearances and actions, Rumfoord can be seen as the champion of outwardness. He has mastered the art of appearing to be superior, so people who base their judgments on appearances believe that he really is superior. But behind his appearance there is little to be found. The religion he creates, "The Church of God the Utterly Indifferent," mirrors his own indifference to the suffering of his fellow human beings. The character of Rumfoord stands as a strong warning against judging people based on appearances. His charm disguises an empty soul capable of heartless cruelty.

Like Rumfoord, Malachi Constant also inherited a large fortune, but he is not a member of the hereditary aristocracy. At his first meeting with Rumfoord he thinks of himself as hopelessly inferior, and readers are invited to share his low opinion of himself. We are told that Rumfoord does everything "*with* style," and therefore makes all of humanity look good, while Constant does everything "*in* style," simply following the corrupt fashions of the times, and so makes humanity look bad (24). Constant's wealth comes from his incredible luck, not intelligence or hard work. He has little education or knowledge of the world and no compassion for others. He uses and discards beautiful women as if they were so many toys that his money can buy. He abuses alcohol and drugs until he is "hardly more respectable" than an animal (49).

But, like all of Vonnegut's characters, Malachi Constant has a few traits that evoke the reader's sympathy. His inability to love may be traced back to his father, whom he saw only once, on his twenty-first birthday. Years later, this lack of attention from his father prompts a fierce need to care for his own son, in spite of all the obstacles. His sense of responsibility for his "mate" Bee and son Chrono mark the beginning of his growth as a character. He writes the first of his letters to himself on Mars to avoid forgetting about Bee and Chrono when his memory is cleaned out. His desire to escape from Mars with them prompts his search for meaning and purpose in the strange Martian environment. This search leads him to a severely limited, but functional, philosophy of life by the end of the novel.

Constant finally gets a chance to be a father to Chrono and a husband to Bee when the three are together on Titan. They are far from a typical family, and each of them lives alone, but they care for one another as best they can. Constant becomes a self-sufficient farmer, and this brings him a great deal of satisfaction. In their old age, he and Beatrice fall in love, and as he explains to Salo after her death, their love taught him a great lesson. "A purpose of human life . . . is to love whoever is around to be loved" (320).

Beatrice Rumfoord is introduced to readers as a wealthy woman of the highest social class who also has some talent as a poet. Our first glimpse of Beatrice is in a formal portrait of her as a child. She is dressed entirely in white and holds the reins of an equally white pony. Malachi Constant decides that the strange look on her face comes from her fear of getting dirty. The portrait is a symbol of the untouchable innocence that Beatrice struggles to preserve by isolating herself from the world. When her husband leaves in his spaceship, she bricks up all entrances to the estate, except for a tiny door, and she allows the formal gardens surrounding the Rumfoord mansion to grow up into a jungle. After she has lost her fortune in the stock market crash, and she is forced to open the mansion to tourists, she looks up at her childhood portrait and consoles herself with the thought that she still has not been "the least bit soiled" (92).

Of course, her immaculate innocence cannot last forever. She is kidnapped by recruiters for the army of Mars, and during the voyage she is raped by Malachi Constant. She suffers through the same memory cleaning that most of the recruits are subjected to, but she struggles to maintain her sense of herself as an independent individual, and she continues to write poetry. The final line of the sonnet she writes on Mars shows that she is still trying to isolate herself from the world: "Yes, every man's an island: island fortress, island home" (153).

Beatrice's stubborn dignity helps her to survive a crash landing in the Amazon jungle and a three-month initiation into the Gumbo tribe. She loses her two front teeth in the crash, and her skin color is permanently darkened by the strange diet of the Gumbos. In a sense, she has been made permanently dirty in a way that would have horrified her only a few years earlier. The next time we see her, she has been reduced to hawking trinkets outside the wall of the mansion she once called home. But in spite of her circumstances, everyone who sees her is impressed by the "grandeur within her" (235). As her husband had predicted, she ends her life "behaving aristocratically" even though she has been stripped of the trappings of aristocracy (60). In her old age on Titan, she returns to her writing and compiles a lengthy refutation of Rumfoord's theory of an indifferent and pointless universe. As she looks once more at the portrait of the impossibly clean little girl, she realizes that "the worst thing that could possibly happen to anybody . . . would be to not be used for anything by anybody" (317). All of her horrible experiences have transformed the innocent girl into a wise old woman.

Boaz, Unk's buddy in the army of Mars, takes a journey through life that is essentially the opposite of Beatrice's. He begins his life immersed in daily struggles with other people and ends it in total isolation in the caves of Mercury. Boaz is an African American orphan who was recruited into the army of Mars when he was just fourteen. As one of the army's "real commanders," he revels in his power to inflict pain on the men he controls, and yet, he shows compassion and concern for his buddy Unk. Although he does not know the details, Boaz does know that his buddy was once fabulously lucky and lived the good life on earth. Boaz plans to use Unk as a guide to the good life, once the Martian army is triumphant. But of course, Boaz's vague dreams about Hollywood nightclubs are never realized. In the caves of Mercury, he has his first opportunity to reflect on his life and what he has learned from it. He realizes that all the while he was in the army, he was being used by an unknown power. His sense of power over others was an illusion. He decides that avoiding fear and loneliness are more important than having power over others. When Unk leaves him to search for a way out of the caves, Boaz focuses his attention on the harmoniums. He learns that he can give them pleasure by playing music and letting them feed on the rhythm of his pulse. When Unk is ready to leave, Boaz decides to stay behind to care for his beloved harmoniums in a place where he can "do good without doing any harm" (217). He dreads the complicated world of human beings, who are so much harder to please. Boaz has achieved the perfect isolation that Beatrice tried so hard to preserve behind the walls of her mansion. But if Boaz has found a paradise where he can lead a blameless existence, look how far he had to go and consider what he had to give up. His refuge is deep inside Mercury, and his only companions are creatures that can feel but cannot think, suggesting that it is impossible to escape from the dirty, complex world where people inevitably hurt one another.

THEMATIC ISSUES

All of the important thematic issues in *The Sirens of Titan* relate to the fundamental distinction, established in the opening pages, between searching for the meaning of life within the soul versus looking to the outside world for answers. The narrator invites readers to adopt the point of view of an observer from the future who already knows that the meaning of life is to be found within the human soul. From this perspective, all religions appear to be "gimcrack" (1). In other words, they have no more value than the plastic trinkets sold near religious shrines. Establishing this perspective allows Vonnegut to embark on a powerful satire of contemporary religions. The novel also deals with a question that is central to most religions: What does it mean to be a good person? Finally, *The Sirens of Titan* picks up the theme of mechanization that Vonnegut explored in *Player Piano* (see chapter 3) and takes it to its logical conclusion.

The Sirens of Titan could be described as a satire on modern religions.

Rather than attacking the beliefs and practices of specific religions, which might disturb readers who identify with them, Vonnegut creates a religion that borrows some of the elements of Judaism and Christianity. Rumfoord establishes his "Church of God the Utterly Indifferent" by staging an enormous spectacle, the suicidal invasion of the earth by a poorly equipped army of brainwashed earthlings from a secret base on Mars. The invasion accomplishes several things. First it creates a feeling of solidarity among all the inhabitants of earth, as they fight together to repel the invaders. Then, as it becomes increasingly apparent that the war is just a slaughter of mindless robots in human form, people begin to feel guilty, and Rumfoord encourages them to see the invaders as saints who martyred themselves for the cause of human brotherhood. The guilt plays the same role in Rumfoord's religion that the concept of original sin does in Christianity, and the Martians become the saints and martyrs of the new religion. Rumfoord solidifies his hold over the popular imagination by performing the "miracle" of predicting future events. The parallels with the miracles performed by Jesus in the gospels are obvious. By showing that Rumfoord's "miracles" are nothing more than tricks designed to fool people into believing in his teachings, Vonnegut suggests that looking for external proof of a spiritual idea makes people vulnerable to manipulation.

Rumfoords' skill as a manipulator of the masses is evident in the spectacle that he hosts to welcome the "Space Wanderer." His mansion is surrounded by stands that sell gimcrack souvenirs, similar to those found near Christian pilgrimage sites such as Lourdes in France. Five minutes before he materializes, a giant steam whistle announces his imminent arrival, and when he actually takes shape, a cannon is fired. When he dematerializes, a thousand balloons are released. Rumfoord has an elaborate stage set and a television audience that would make a contemporary televangelist envious. More importantly, he knows what the crowd wants and how to give it to them. As he explains to Malachi Constant, the Space Wanderer, people love the "thrill of the *fast reverse*," from good fortune to bad, or vice versa (252). Actually, Rumfoord has a double reverse in mind for Constant, from the bad fortune of his time on Mars and Mercury, to his triumphant return as the Space Wanderer, and then back to bad luck, as his identity is revealed and he is sent into exile on Titan. Rumfoord has already made Malachi Constant into a "central symbol of wrong-headedness" and an example of all the mistakes that human beings have made throughout history (260). He becomes a scapegoat for the new religion by taking the sins of the faithful into space with him, just as the ancient Hebrews symbolically transferred their sins to a goat and then turned it loose in the wilderness (see the biblical book of Leviticus, chapter 16). By describing Rumfoord's church, Vonnegut satirizes the methods that real religions use to manipulate their members. All of the pageants and spectacles distract people from looking within and discovering the meaning of their lives in their own souls.

The Sirens of Titan takes up an issue that is central to religious thought: What does it mean to be a good person? For Beatrice, at the beginning of the novel, it means remaining untouched by life, in a state of perpetual innocence. But the novel shows that it is impossible to remain innocent forever, and even if it were possible, a life in total isolation from others would not really be a life at all. It would be easy to brand Malachi Constant a sinner, regardless of one's religion, but like most people, he considers himself a victim of larger forces rather than a villain. But after his rape of Beatrice, he realizes "that he was not only a victim of outrageous fortune, but one of outrageous fortune's cruellest agents as well" (163). As critic Tony Tanner has pointed out, all of the novel's characters play the dual role of victim/agent, and so do the characters in the rest of Vonnegut's fiction. Vonnegut's father once pointed out to him that there are no real villains in his stories, and Vonnegut replied that there were no real heroes either (*Slaughterhouse-Five* 10). All of his characters live in a morally ambiguous world where an action that seems to be good may have terrible consequences and where the worst people have some redeeming traits. Absolute good or evil is impossible, but that does not mean that there are no standards of behavior. Once Malachi Constant becomes aware of himself as a victim/agent, he begins to study "the intricate tactics of causing less rather than more pain" (163). In Vonnegut's world, this limited definition of goodness is the highest possible goal.

The Sirens of Titan picks up the theme of mechanization that was central to *Player Piano* and takes it to its logical conclusion (for a discussion of mechanization in *Player Piano*, see chapter 3). Salo, Rumfoord's companion on Titan, is from the planet Tralfamadore, where there are no living creatures, just machines. The machines have a legend to explain where they came from, and it is a potent satire on human beings' preoccupation with finding the meaning of life outside themselves. According to the legend, Tralfamadore was once populated by creatures who, unlike machines, were not "efficient ... predictable ... [or] durable" (279). These creatures were constantly searching for their purpose, but whenever they found a purpose, it seemed "so low that the creatures were filled with disgust and shame" (279). They designed machines to serve these lower purposes while they continued to search for higher ones. Eventually they assigned the task of finding their highest purpose to the machines. The machines were programmed to be truthful, so they were bound to say that the creatures really had no purpose at all. "[B]ecause they hated purposeless things above all else," they began killing one another, and finally, they called on their machines to finish the job. In the context of the novel, this story functions as a parable to show readers the folly of looking for the meaning of life outside themselves. Machines can be made to serve many useful purposes, but they can never answer the big questions that make human life interesting. *The Sirens of Titan* challenges readers to think about these questions for themselves rather than looking to machines, or religious leaders, for answers.

A STRUCTURALIST READING

Structuralists are less concerned with *what* a particular work of literature says than they are in *how* it conveys its meaning. Structuralism began with the work of Ferdinand de Saussure (1857–1913) who is considered the father of modern linguistics, the scientific study of language. According to Saussure, each language is governed by its own set of rules that determine which sounds speakers use, how those sounds are combined into words, and how the words are put together to create meaningful sentences. Saussure pointed out that words do not have any direct connection to the things that they stand for. The word "cat" is a combination of letters that indicate certain sounds, but there is no reason to suppose that those letters and sounds are the only ones that can be used to make you think of a cat. In fact, in other languages, different words do the job just as well. If you say *gato* to a Spanish speaker, or *chat* to a French speaker, they will both think of a cat, but if you say "cat," they will be baffled. So if there is no direct connection between the words we use and the ideas that we are trying to express, how does language work? Saussure answers by saying that words are actually signs made up of two parts, the signified and the signifier. The signified is the concept that is conveyed by the signifier, letters on a page or sounds made in speaking. Therefore, when you say "cat," the sound is the signifier; when you write it, the letters are the signifier; either way the idea of a cat that comes to your friend's mind is the signified. The signs that are created by the combination of signifier and signified acquire meaning from their relationships with other signs in the language. We know the meaning of "cat" because it differs from "dog," and from all the other signs in the language. Structuralists, believing that language is composed of signs arranged according to rules, set out to discover the rules that govern human communication.

When the basic ideas of structuralism are applied to literature, they lead to some surprising insights. Because structuralists believe that works of literature, like individual signs in the language, get their meaning from their relationships with other texts, they often point out interesting connections between different texts and explore how each influences the meaning of the other. This reciprocal relationship between texts is called "intertextuality." When structuralists discover a text that has a relationship with another, they call it an "intertext." Structuralists believe that works of literature also create meaning by using the basic building blocks of language, pairs of opposites such as light/darkness, up/down, good/bad. These are known as "binary oppositions" because each consists of two parts (*bi* comes from the Latin for "two"). Each member of a binary opposition gets its meaning from contrast with the other member, and in each pair, one member is more highly valued. For instance, we know what "light" means because we contrast it with "darkness," and people have learned to value light more than darkness. The more highly valued element in a binary opposition is referred to as the "privileged" one, while the other is "unprivileged." When people read a work of literature, they use their knowledge of binary oppositions, and the values associated with them, to decide what the text means. Structuralists identify the most important binary oppositions in a particular work and examine how they help the work achieve its meaning. They often find that a brief passage provides a key that unlocks the structure of the entire work.

To look at *The Sirens of Titan* from a structuralist point of view, one must identify the most important binary oppositions in the text and consider how Vonnegut uses these to convey meaning. One must also look for cases of intertexuality, where Vonnegut refers to other texts in order to create meaning. A detailed examination of a brief passage on the copyright page at the front of the book will provide the key that unlocks the structure of the entire novel: "All persons, places, and events in this book are real. Certain speeches and thoughts are necessarily constructions by the author. No names have been changed to protect the innocent, since God Almighty protects the innocent as a matter of Heavenly routine." The first two sentences in this statement use the binary opposition between reality and fiction ("real" / "constructions"). In this opposition, reality is more highly valued than fiction. It is linked with truth as opposed to falsehood and to experience as opposed to imagination. By claiming that everything in his book is real, Vonnegut is trying to place it on the privileged side of the binary opposition. But this statement itself is an obvious falsehood. Although real places are mentioned, the characters are inventions and the events are improbable, to say the least. No one is likely to be fooled into believing that this book describes actual events. So how does this statement contribute to the novel's meaning? For one thing it calls into question the values usually associated with the opposition between reality and fiction. If Vonnegut's book is real, then what we call reality is actually a fiction, a story that we tell ourselves. By calling his story real, he forces us to ask, "What is real?" The standard answer would be something like "true to the facts of human experience" or "verifiable by science." But works of fiction may be true to the *spirit* of human experience even if they disregard scientific notions of fact.

This insight leads us to one of the central binary oppositions that give the book its structure. Vonnegut takes the fundamental distinction between in and out and reverses the normal relationship between them. Most people consider reality something outside of themselves. What is inside is somehow less real. It is subjective rather than objective, associated with feelings rather than facts. As Vonnegut points out in the opening pages, human beings would rather look outside themselves for answers than look within. The narrator says clearly that this is a mistake, and we must reverse the opposition so that the inward quest becomes privileged. The rest of the novel is an extended proof of the folly of looking outward, but its meaning depends on the binary opposition established in the opening pages.

The full meaning of the statement on the copyright page also depends on the reader recognizing two intertexts. One is the traditional "Publisher's Note" that is often found on the copyright page of novels in order to protect the author from libel suits. A typical disclaimer takes this form: "This is a work of fiction. Names, characters, places, and incidents either are the product of the author's imagination or are used fictitiously, and any resemblance to actual persons, living or dead, events, or locales, is entirely coincidental." Readers who are expecting the traditional disclaimer will be surprised to see that Vonnegut has turned it on its head. In this way, he warns his readers to expect the unexpected and to take his surprises seriously. A second intertext is the 1950s television show *Dragnet*, a police drama that was based on true stories. Every show began with a voice announcing, "What you are about to see is true. The names have been changed to protect the innocent." Of course, all police dramas are concerned with questions of guilt and innocence, and so is Vonnegut's novel. But in *The Sirens of Titan*, Vonnegut questions the validity of this binary opposition and shows that in real life such simple distinctions do not hold up (see the discussion of the victim/agent opposition in the section on thematic issues).

The statement on the copyright page throws readers off balance at the start, and Vonnegut does his best to keep them off balance throughout the novel because he wants them to question their most basic values. If readers look at the book as a space fantasy with no connection to their everyday lives, they are likely to miss its serious message. Although the people and events in the book are not real in the conventional sense, they provide readers with insights into human behavior that are truer and more significant than those to be found in any reality-based television show.

Mother Night
(1961)

Mother Night is Kurt Vonnegut's most challenging and perhaps his most frequently misunderstood novel. Howard W. Campbell, Jr., the novel's protagonist, is an American who broadcasts Nazi propaganda during the Second World War. But Campbell is also a valuable spy for the Allies, so it is impossible to simply condemn him as a Nazi collaborator. Instead, the novel presents multiple perspectives on the question of Campbell's guilt or innocence and shows that society's judgment is often arbitrary. Vonnegut's refusal to judge his characters makes it difficult to know where he stands, but more importantly, it forces readers to consider how they make moral judgments.

Mother Night is the first Vonnegut novel to deal directly with the Second World War, and it challenges the commonly accepted version of the war as a battle between good and evil by showing that the real moral battleground is inside every human being. Bernard B. O'Hare, the American soldier who captures Campbell at the end of the war, is so obsessed with punishing him that he becomes as cold and ruthless as the most fanatical Nazi. The novel also challenges America's sense of moral superiority by presenting native-born Nazis as simply the latest manifestation of American racism.

Mother Night is also the first of Vonnegut's novels written in the first person. It includes an editor's introduction signed by "Kurt Vonnegut, Jr." that describes the novel as "the American edition of the confessions of Howard W. Campbell, Jr." (ix). The introduction is obviously a lie.

This is a novel, not the confessions of a notorious Nazi, but by making the claim that this is a true story, Vonnegut calls into question our ability to distinguish between truth and falsehood. Vonnegut, posing as Campbell's editor, points out that because he was a dramatist, Campbell was also a liar, someone who was willing to reshape the world to make it fit in his plays. But he goes on to argue that artistic lying can be a way to a higher form of truth. By letting a professional liar like Campbell tell his own story, Vonnegut challenges the reader to distinguish between truth and lies, and then to think about how lies can reveal deeper truths. As a playwright, Campbell created roles for others to play on the stage. During the war, he played the role of a Nazi in real life. *Mother Night* examines the consequences of role-playing and demonstrates that people often become the roles they play.

PLOT DEVELOPMENT

Mother Night is told in the first person by the novel's protagonist, Howard W. Campbell, Jr. As the novel opens, Campbell is in an Israeli prison awaiting trial for war crimes and writing his "confessions," so they may be added to an archive on Nazi war criminals. Although the novel is presented as Campbell's "confessions," it is far from a simple acknowledgement of guilt. Less than 20 percent of the book deals with the war years, and most of these passages are descriptions of other people rather than accounts of Campbell's own activities. To complicate matters further, Campbell does not tell his story in chronological order. Instead of beginning with an explanation of why he became a Nazi or with a description of his early years, Campbell tells the stories of the four Jewish guards who watch him around the clock. On a first reading, telling the war stories of his guards rather than his own appears to be a delaying tactic brought on by Campbell's reluctance to acknowledge his "crimes against humanity" (29). However, a second reading reveals that these stories provide four different contexts for Campbell's own story, and each one reminds the reader how difficult it is to determine the guilt or innocence of individuals caught up in the madness of war. The guard's stories will be discussed in detail in the section on themes.

Campbell's conversations with the guards evoke his memories in an order that sometimes seems random but that closer inspection reveals to be artful. On the first page, he refers to himself as "a Nazi by reputation," which leaves open the possibility that he might not have been a Nazi in fact. Speaking to one of the guards, he admits that he broadcast anti-

Semitic propaganda on the radio, but the guard, who reads a transcript of one of his speeches, points out that it is pretty mild in comparison to what others were saying at the time. These opening chapters establish a pattern in which Campbell admits to a crime and then immediately makes it seem less serious by showing how his guards react to it. He seems to be attempting to lessen his guilt in the eyes of the reader, and yet, he withholds the single piece of information that is most likely to win the reader's sympathy—that he was an American agent who only pretended to be a Nazi. Not until he has described his fifteen years of hiding in New York after the war and given a very brief sketch of his life does he reveal that he was a spy.

Chapter 7 of the novel is titled "Autobiography," and in it, Campbell gives a four-page overview of his life, beginning with his birth in Schenectady, New York, in 1912. His father was an engineer with General Electric, and when Howard was eleven, his job took the family to Berlin where Howard completed his education, married a German woman, and became a popular playwright. When the war started, his parents returned to the United States, but Howard and his wife stayed and became involved with the Nazis. Campbell wrote and broadcast Nazi propaganda in English, and as the war was ending, he was caught by an American lieutenant, Bernard B. O'Hare, and charged with war crimes.

Up to this point, Campbell has not revealed that he was an American agent, so his guilt seems beyond question, but in the next chapter, he describes his first meeting with Major Frank Wirtanen of the U.S. War Department in Berlin in 1938. Wirtanen convinces Campbell to become a spy by telling him a story about a young American who has lived in Germany almost long enough to be considered German, but who, when war comes, decides to use his connections with the Nazis to become a valuable American agent. Of course, Campbell realizes that Wirtanen is talking about him, and he refuses, but Wirtanen, who has read Campbell's plays, knows how to appeal to his deepest desires. He points out that, as a spy, Campbell would be an "authentic hero," although no one would know of his heroism (38). Wirtanen admits that if Campbell survives the war he will be considered a traitor to his country and have little reason to go on living, but he is not concerned that this admission will dissuade Campbell from becoming a spy. On the contrary, Wirtanen's story of Campbell's life as a spy is calculated to appeal to the idealism that is revealed in his plays. Wirtanen knows that Campbell "admire[s] pure hearts and heroes" and that he "believe[s] in romance" (39). Campbell adds an even better reason of his own. He is a "ham" and being a spy allows him to turn his entire life into a play in which he is the star. He does such a good job of pretending to be a Nazi that no one suspects "the honest me" concealed within (39). This distinction between the role he played and his hidden, authentic, innocent self is his best defense against the war crimes he is charged with, but the novel as a whole makes it clear that by pretending to be a Nazi Campbell actually became one. His insistence on a true identity distinct from the role he played is a symptom of schizophrenia, a split-personality disorder.

Although his love for his German wife Helga sustained Campbell amid the madness of war, he never told her that he was a spy. He claims that he withheld the truth, not to protect himself, but to protect her from one more worry. In public, they were the embodiment of Nazi patriotism, but in private, they retreated to a separate world, a "nation of two" where war and propaganda could not reach them (42). Helga was lost while entertaining German troops, and the detective agency Campbell hired after the war could never prove whether she was alive or dead.

After the war, Campbell's life continues to revolve around Helga. His rat-infested attic in New York becomes a shrine to her memory, and for thirteen years, he avoids contact with other people. Then one day he purchases a wood carving kit, makes a chess set, and knocks on a neighbor's door, hoping to find someone who will play with him. The man behind the door, George Kraft, is also a loner anxious for a little company. Although Campbell does not discover it for years, he tells the reader immediately that Kraft is really Iona Potapov, a Russian spy. The two men become close friends, and eventually Campbell reveals what he did during the war. Kraft expresses his outrage at the way the U.S. government has treated Campbell, but at the same time, he is plotting to use Campbell to help the Russians in the propaganda battle that was an important part of the cold war. He notifies *The White Christian Minuteman*, an American Nazi newspaper, that Campbell is living in obscurity in New York. To ensure that word of Campbell's whereabouts reaches a wider audience, Kraft suggests that they send a copy of the paper to Bernard B. O'Hare, the man who captured Campbell at the end of the war. O'Hare responds with a threatening letter to Campbell, and he sends copies to the F.B.I., *Time, Newsweek,* and other publications.

Once Campbell's hiding place is revealed, the plot begins to move at a faster pace. Lionel Jones, founder and publisher of *The White Christian Minuteman*, visits Campbell along with a motley gang of paranoid racists who revere Campbell for his work with the Nazis. They claim to have found Campbell's long lost wife Helga, and in spite of her suspiciously youthful appearance, Campbell believes that she really is Helga. At first the two are shy with one another, but after "Helga" tells the long story of her years as a prisoner and slave in Eastern Europe, their romance is rekindled, and they spend a passionate night together in a hotel. The next morning they pledge their eternal love for one another, and "Helga" reveals that she is really Resi, Helga's younger sister, who was only ten years old the last time Campbell saw her. Initially the news devastates Campbell, but when Resi explains that she loved him even as a child, and that thoughts of him were all that sustained her through years of forced labor, Campbell decides to continue pretending that she is really Helga. But Resi does not want to go on playing the role of her sister, so she begins to reveal her own personality in hopes that Campbell will love her for who she really is. She encourages him to write again so that she may star in his plays by acting out the "quintessence of Resi," just as once he wrote plays so that Helga could reveal her true self (139). However, now that Campbell's existence has been revealed to the world, the lovers will not be allowed to lead the quiet life that they long for.

When they return to Campbell's building, they are confronted by an irate veteran intent on punishing Campbell for his war crimes. The man beats Campbell until he loses consciousness. When he awakes, he finds himself in the basement of Lionel Jones's house, surrounded by Nazi emblems, including a portrait of Hitler over the mantelpiece. The basement is the headquarters of the "Iron Guard of the White Sons of the American Constitution," a fascist youth group sponsored by Jones's neo-Nazi organization (150). Resi explains that this was the only place she could think of where Campbell would be safe. Surrounded by all these reminders of his Nazi past, Campbell reflects on the influence his broadcasts had. His protectors still believe all the lies he told so long ago. They even take target practice by shooting at a grotesque caricature of a Jewish banker that Campbell drew during the war. Campbell does not deny his participation in the Nazi madness, but he claims that he always tried to exaggerate his propaganda so much that no sane person could believe it. Unfortunately, as Campbell has learned too late, the world is full of people who have no sense of the ridiculous, who are "incapable of thought," and who are ready to believe the worst about others (160). Campbell blames his audience for believing what he said in order to evade responsibility for his words, but from another point of view, he has correctly diagnosed the collective madness that made the Nazi era possible.

While Campbell was unconscious, Resi and Kraft planned an escape to Mexico on a small plane owned by a friend of Jones. They describe an idyllic life of creativity in a tropical paradise, safe from those who

are determined to punish Campbell for his war crimes. During a me-
morial service for one of Jones's men, someone slips Campbell a note
that warns him that he is in danger. Following the directions in the note,
Campbell enters an abandoned building where he meets with Frank Wirtanen for the last time.

Wirtanen reveals that Kraft is really Iona Potapov, a Russian agent,
and that Resi is an East German agent. Only the second revelation is a
surprise to the reader, but it is all news to Campbell, and his world is
shattered. Wirtanen says that the pair planned to take him to Mexico
and then fly immediately to Moscow where Campbell would be tried as
a war criminal and forced to make a false confession about collaboration
between the United States and the Nazis before and after the war. If
Campbell refused, the Russians would threaten to kill his beloved Resi.
Wirtanen warns Campbell that he must not return to Jones's house because it is about to be raided, but Campbell can think of nowhere else
to go. Even though he knows that his best friend and his lover are merely
using him, he is unwilling to give up the fantasy of a quiet, artistic life
with them. Yet neither can he hide his new knowledge from them, and
he slowly reveals that he knows about their plot by playfully suggesting
that they change their plans and go to Moscow. Resi denies that she was
going to betray him, even as she admits to being an East German agent,
and she proves her pure love for Campbell by committing suicide before
the F.B.I. agents can take her into custody. Her final words include
quotes from one of Campbell's' plays, and she claims that if she cannot
live for love, she has no reason to go on living. Kraft/Potapov submits
quietly to the authorities. Even when they mock his disastrous career as
a spy, he claims that he does not care because he is really a painter, and
all his other identities are unimportant to him.

Campbell is once again allowed to escape, but he does not get very
far. Walking down the street, he suddenly freezes because he no longer
has any reason to go anywhere. He realizes that mere "curiosity" kept
him moving through life for years, and now even curiosity has deserted
him (232). Finally a police officer asks him to move along, and he finds
himself walking mechanically toward his old building. Upstairs in his
attic room, Campbell finds Bernard B. O'Hare waiting for him. O'Hare
is dressed in his American Legion uniform, and he is very drunk. In his
mind, he is Saint George and Campbell is the dragon, a figure of pure
evil. When he attacks, Campbell breaks his arm with a pair of fire tongs
and then lectures him on the folly of attempting to fight pure evil. Campbell says that although there are "reasons for fighting" there is "no good
reason ever to hate without reservation" or to imagine that God shares

your hatred (251). He then chases O'Hare from the building and knocks on the door of Dr. Jacob Epstein, an Auschwitz survivor, to ask that Epstein turn him over to the Israeli authorities so that he may stand trial. At first Epstein refuses, arguing that he is not an agent of the Israeli government and that he does not want revenge for what happened to him at Auschwitz. But Epstein's mother is also a survivor, and she does want revenge. She calls three men who agree to watch Campbell and turn him over to the Israelis in the morning.

The final chapter returns Campbell to the Israeli prison where the novel began. Many witnesses are set to testify against him, but the most damning evidence will come from recordings of his own wartime broadcasts. Campbell's lawyer pins all his hopes on some new evidence arriving in the mail, and against all odds, a letter from Frank Wirtanen arrives the day before the trial. In it Wirtanen reveals his true name and confirms that Campbell was a spy for the United States during the war. Although this letter is his ticket to freedom, Campbell is not relieved when he reads it. The novel ends with Campbell planning to hang himself, not for his crimes against humanity, but for "crimes against himself" (268).

CHARACTER DEVELOPMENT

Howard W. Campbell, Jr., is the only well-developed character in *Mother Night*. The minor characters that surround Campbell act like mirrors, highlighting different aspects of his personality. When Campbell describes them he is also describing parts of himself. As the novel progresses, it becomes clear that Campbell is interested in other people only to the extent that they provide him with insights into his own personality.

Campbell's character must have been shaped by his parents, but he offers only a few clues about their influence on him. His father, an engineer for General Electric, is so devoted to his job that he has little time for his son. Outside of work, his only interest is in a photographic history of the First World War. Because he forbids his son to look at the book, young Howard pores over it every chance he gets, immersing himself in images of dead and mutilated bodies. Howard's mother is a talented cellist with a "morbid" personality (26). Howard, an only child, is her "principal companion" until he is nearly ten years old. One night in their darkened kitchen, she mixes rubbing alcohol and salt, lights it to produce a yellow flame, and tells Howard that the strange light shows them as they will look when they are dead. This bizarre incident scares both mother and son so much that it ends their close relationship. At the age of ten, Howard finds himself estranged from his parents. Both of them have encouraged his morbid fascination with death, and their withdrawal produces in Howard a detachment from other people that makes it difficult for him to sympathize with others later in life. The suffering that surrounds him during World War II is no more real to him than the pictures in his father's book, pictures that he describes casually as "the usual furniture of world wars" (26).

Estranged from both parents, eleven-year-old Howard is ready to immerse himself in German culture when the family moves to Berlin in 1923. Living in Germany gives him a chance to discard his troubled childhood and embrace a way of life that is forever foreign to his parents. His marriage to the beautiful and talented Helga and his success as a playwright strengthen his ties to his adopted country.

Campbell's plays provide important clues to his character. Set in the Middle Ages and peopled with characters who stand for abstract notions like purity and love, the plays seem to be detached from the political and social issues of the twentieth century. As Frank Wirtanen points out, they reveal Campbell to be a person who believes in pure good and evil and who trusts in the redemptive power of love. He seems hopelessly naive, but the novel will not allow readers to dismiss his naiveté as a harmless, even charming, fault. For one thing, the Nazis love his plays and so does Josef Stalin, the Soviet dictator and mass-murderer. Even though on the surface Campbell's plays appear to have nothing to do with politics, they reinforce the simplistic and dangerous notion that some people are all good while others are purely evil. Hitler and Stalin both believed they were good and their enemies were evil, and they used this belief to justify mass murder. In this light, Campbell's assertion that his plays are nonpolitical is seen as another dangerous delusion.

Campbell's most serious delusion is that he can play the part of a Nazi while maintaining the purity of a "true" self, hidden behind the role. From the moment that Wirtanen recruits him, he imagines that he is acting, but life is not a play, and those who suffered and died at the hands of the Nazis will not come to life again when the curtain falls. Campbell says that he suffers from "schizophrenia" (179). The literal meaning of the word is "splitting of the mind," and this is a good description of a condition that allows Campbell to be a convincing Nazi while maintaining a sense of his own virtue.

Campbell exhibits several symptoms that are typical of schizophrenics. The *Review of General Psychiatry* describes schizophrenic patients as having "lost touch with who they are," and this certainly applies to

Campbell, who complains of "several selves" coexisting uneasily within one body (184). Suffering from a lack of energy, blunted emotions, and an inability to experience pleasure, schizophrenics often withdraw from society. After the war, Campbell experiences all of these symptoms as he lives alone and friendless in his attic apartment. As the illness progresses, some schizophrenics lose all interest in life, and they may remain motionless for long periods. Near the end of the novel, Campbell freezes twice because he is unable to decide where to go or what to do, and he even applies the clinical term "catalepsis" to his condition (256).

The *Review of General Psychiatry* points out that schizophrenia is difficult to diagnose because all of its symptoms are also symptoms of other disorders, and not all sufferers exhibit all of the classic symptoms. Still, it must be pointed out that Campbell functions at a very high level throughout the war years. He does not suffer from an inability to concentrate, nor does he exhibit the severe disturbances in thought and language that usually make it impossible for untreated schizophrenics to function normally in society. Nor does he suffer from delusions about powerful forces out to get him, as many schizophrenics do, even though after the war, he is wanted by the Israeli government. These inconsistencies suggest that Vonnegut is using the term "schizophrenia" loosely. He is not trying to diagnose Campbell but rather to use the general idea of a "splitting of the mind" to explain how someone could be a Nazi and still think of himself as a good person.

Vonnegut stretches the definition of schizophrenia even further by calling it a "widespread boon to modern mankind" (179). Psychologists estimate that approximately one percent of the population suffers from schizophrenia, which makes it one of the most common mental illnesses but hardly justifies calling it "widespread." Obviously, schizophrenia is not a good thing, so calling it a "boon" is ironic, but Vonnegut is calling attention to the ability that many people develop to divide their lives into neat compartments as a way of living with their faults and failings. Campbell is a master at this compartmentalization, and it allows him to live with his crimes for many years. Ultimately, Campbell gives himself up to the Israelis because he can no longer bear to live as a divided self. His final words make it clear that he plans to commit suicide, not because of overwhelming guilt for crimes against humanity, but instead because of his "crimes against himself" (268). It is important to note that he does not say, "I plan to kill myself for crimes against myself." Instead he uses the third person, "himself," showing that he still suffers from the "splitting of the mind" that made his career as a spy possible.

Campbell is a complex, deeply troubled character who manages to engage the reader's sympathy even as he confesses to horrible crimes. He is a victim of the madness of the twentieth century, and he is also an agent, spreading that madness to others and promoting irrational hatred.

The novel's minor characters act like mirrors that reflect different aspects of Campbell's personality. The Russian spy Iona Potapov, alias George Kraft, is the most obvious example. Like Campbell, Kraft is an artist whose greatest satisfaction comes from his craft, which makes his alias appropriate. Kraft convinces Campbell that he is a sincere friend, and Campbell maintains this conviction even after Kraft has attempted to betray him. Campbell chalks up the apparent contradiction to the schizophrenia that allows Kraft to be a good friend and a ruthless spy at the same time (53). Of course, Campbell suffers from the same disorder and reflecting on Kraft's actions helps him realize it. But before Campbell discovers that he is a spy, Kraft rekindles Campbell's interest in art. He speaks passionately about the supreme importance of art and the artist's obligation to be productive and leave a legacy for future generations. Although it is as difficult to determine Kraft's "true" character as it is to pin down Campbell's, these sentiments seem sincere. At the end of the novel, when his plot to kidnap Campbell has failed, he defends himself by declaring that his incompetence as a spy does not matter because he is really a painter. Campbell comments that this is an example of Kraft's schizophrenia coming to his rescue, but ironically his capture allows Kraft to escape the splitting of the mind that plagues Campbell to the end. In fact, Kraft's failure as a spy leads to his triumph as an artist. Free from all distractions, he continues to paint in federal prison, and he finally achieves the recognition that he could not seek when he was a spy. Although Kraft is not a well-rounded character in his own right, he calls attention to Campbell's "spy schizophrenia" and to his failure to remain true to his art.

Resi Noth, the younger sister of Campbell's wife Helga and his lover in the heady weeks before their capture, is also a spy who retains a greater degree of integrity than Campbell does. Although she deceives Campbell into thinking that she is Helga in order to get him to fall in love with her, in the end she proves the sincerity of her love by committing suicide rather than allowing herself to be separated from Campbell. Resi was a young girl during the war, and she learned not to hope for much in life. When Campbell arrives to shoot her pet dog, Resi does not care, nor does she care that she and everyone she knows will likely die soon. Campbell calls her a "nihilist," and it seems that she does not believe in anything, but a fantasy that she will someday marry Campbell and that he will write plays for her sustains her through the difficult years after the war (108). Her mission as a spy allows her to realize part of this fantasy, but ultimately she must choose between loyalty to Campbell and loyalty to the East German government. Her suicide proves that she would rather end her life like a heroine in one of Campbell's plays than give up her sustaining belief in true love. Like Campbell and Kraft, Resi lives as if she were playing a role, but unlike the men, she sticks to her part rather than abandoning it for another more convenient one when circumstances change.

THEMATIC ISSUES

As the "Editor's Note" explains, the title *Mother Night* comes from a speech by Mephistopheles, a devil in Goethe's *Faust*, a classic play from German literature. The speech provides a useful introduction to the novel's principal themes. Mephistopheles claims to be part of "Mother Night, . . . the darkness that gave birth to light" (xii). He describes a battle between light and darkness that is also a battle between good and evil. However, he points out that light and darkness are really inseparable. Light can never break free from darkness, and it is impossible to perceive one without the other. This is also an accurate description of the moral universe of Vonnegut's novel. *Mother Night* presents characters and situations in which good and evil are so thoroughly mixed that it is impossible to separate them, which forces readers to question what we mean by guilt and innocence, good and evil.

Mephistopheles's speech is also his introduction to Faust, in which he reveals important details about his identity while concealing others. Mephistopheles, like Campbell, is unreliable. He is like an actor creating a role that will appeal to Faust, just as Campbell played the role of a Nazi during the war. The novel's second major theme is the uncertainty of personal identity in a world where everyone plays many parts. Is Campbell a Nazi or an American hero? How can we be sure about the identities of even our closest friends when we remain mysteries to ourselves?

The impending trial of Howard W. Campbell, Jr., raises important questions about guilt and innocence. Although Campbell freely admits his involvement with the Nazis and acknowledges the evil actions inspired by his hateful words, he claims that everything he did actually helped the Allies win the war. His words were pure evil, but the pauses between the words conveyed vital information that ultimately led to the triumph of good over evil. Is it possible to separate the good from the evil and weigh one against the other on the scales of justice? *Mother Night* suggests that it is foolish and ultimately meaningless to try. The chaos of a world at war mixes good and evil so thoroughly that even the wisdom of Solomon could not untangle them. Campbell actually invokes the memory of Solomon early in the novel when he remarks that his brand-new prison contains some stones cut in Solomon's time. History surrounds Campbell, but it provides no reliable standards by which he can be judged. Instead, the novel creates multiple perspectives on the question of Campbell's guilt or innocence, beginning with the Israeli guards who watch him around the clock.

The first guard Campbell describes is Arnold Marx, who is too young to remember the war. An amateur archeologist obsessed with the history of Hazor, an ancient city that he is excavating, Marx has never heard of Joseph Goebbels, one of the most notorious Nazis, but he can lecture at length on Tiglath Pileser the Third, an Assyrian king who reigned 2,700 years ago. He is not interested in World War II, but he tells Campbell about a holocaust that was committed by the ancient Israelites, who killed all 40,000 residents of Hazor when they captured it around 1400 B.C.E. Marx helps Campbell put his own story in the context of world history, where it becomes just another atrocity in a long and ever expanding list. The young man's lack of interest in World War II reminds Campbell that soon his story will be part of ancient history, remembered only by a few specialists.

The guard who comes on duty after Marx, Andor Gutman, is an Auschwitz survivor who volunteered to escort Jews to the gas chambers and put their bodies in the ovens, even though he knew that he would be killed as soon as the last body burned. He cannot understand why he and many others volunteered for this gruesome work, but he insists that it was "shameful" (9). As a Jew who was imprisoned at Auschwitz, Gutman was certainly a victim of the Nazis, but he also collaborated with them. His story suggests that it is possible to be a victim and a villain at the same time, and this is how Campbell chooses to portray himself in his confessions (for other characters who are both victim and villain, see the discussion of the "victim/agent" in chapter 4).

The third guard, Arpad Kovacs, escaped the concentration camps by acquiring false identity papers and joining the *Schutzstaffel*, or S.S., the most feared branch of Nazism. Like Campbell, he played a role in order to survive, and he did it so well that he was put in charge of a special unit to find out who was giving information to the Jews. Although Kovacs was the source of the leaks, he was such a "pure and terrifying

Aryan" that no one suspected him (13). Kovacs's story is quite similar to Campbell's, and it provides the best reasons for excusing Campbell's collaboration with the Nazis. Like Kovacs, Campbell was a spy, and he provided valuable information to the Allies, but in order to be effective as a spy, he had to become a convincing Nazi. When Kovacs reads a transcript of one of Campbell's radio broadcasts, he is disappointed and claims that he would not have tolerated anyone in his S.S. platoon who spoke in such a "friendly way about the Jews" (13). Presumably, as an S.S. officer, Kovacs participated in the atrocities committed against his fellow Jews, but far from feeling remorse for his actions, he has nothing but scorn for those who submitted to the Nazis and went quietly to the gas chambers. In a very real sense, Kovacs's guilt is greater than Campbell's, and yet Kovacs is the guard and Campbell the prisoner. Why? Simply because Campbell's crimes were committed in public and because the U.S. government refused to acknowledge that he was an American agent. Comparing Campbell to Kovacs shows how arbitrary society's decisions about guilt and innocence often are.

The last of Campbell's four guards is Bernard Mengel, and his story highlights the moral numbness that the war caused in many survivors. He claims that Campbell is the only one he has ever met who has a guilty conscience about what he did in the war. Even Rudolph Hoess, the commandant of Auschwitz, had no trouble sleeping as he awaited his execution. Mengel says that he was so numbed by the horrors of war that he felt no different fastening a strap around Hoess's ankles before he was hanged and putting a strap around his suitcase less than an hour later. Once again, the guard's story sheds a favorable light on Campbell. At least Campbell acknowledges guilt and claims to feel remorse for the hateful propaganda he broadcast during the war.

Taken together, the four stories of Campbell's guards can be read as his sly, subtle attempt to excuse his actions and win the readers' sympathy. But even readers who are aware that they are being manipulated must admit that in the early pages of his confessions Campbell has succeeded in calling into question the neat classifications of victim/villain and innocence/guilt.

Of course, Campbell criticizes his Nazi bosses, calling them "ignorant and insane," and showing their lack of human sympathy, but he is careful not to demonize them (69). Recalling the days before the war when his plays were popular with the Nazis, he admits that, although he and his wife were not "crazy about Nazis," they didn't hate them either (36). Even reflecting on them after the war, after he has seen the death camps, he cannot "think of them as trailing slime behind" because he "knew them too well as people" (36). The Nazis considered their victims sub-human. *Mother Night* insists on the humanity of these victims, but it also insists on the humanity of the Nazis because as soon as we deny the humanity of any group we fall into the same way of thinking that made Nazism possible.

Mother Night also attacks the dangerous delusion that Nazism was an essentially German phenomenon that arose from some fundamental flaw in the German people. Vonnegut's introduction to the novel begins by mentioning the "native American Fascists" that he knew as a boy in Indianapolis and goes on to describe the Allied firebombing of Dresden, which killed 135,000 German civilians in a single night (v). American Nazis figure prominently in the novel, and their links to the Ku Klux Klan remind readers that hate groups have a long history in the United States. Even more devastating to American notions of moral superiority is the novel's portrait of Bernard B. O'Hare, who is as filled with hatred and as convinced of his own righteousness as any Nazi. For O'Hare, Campbell is the embodiment of pure evil, but Campbell points out that evil is in everyone: "It's that large part of every man that wants to hate without limit, that wants to hate with God on its side" (251). *Mother Night* challenges the commonly accepted version of World War II as a battle between good and evil by showing that the real moral battleground is inside every human being. The novel suggests that we try to determine guilt and innocence as a way of avoiding the more significant and difficult question of how to live with fragmented selves that are aware of both good and evil impulses. Andor Gutman tells Campbell that if he could write a book that would explain why he and other Auschwitz prisoners volunteered to carry corpses for the Nazis, it would be "a very great book" (8). *Mother Night* does not answer this question, but it does explore the mixed motives that lie behind all human actions.

The shift from an external to an internal battle leads us to the second major theme of *Mother Night*, the question of personal identity. Presented as "The Confessions of Howard W. Campbell, Jr." the novel promises to reveal Campbell's character in depth and establish his true identity. Instead it raises more questions than it answers, suggesting that human identities are not unified and coherent but merely the sum of all the different roles we choose to play.

By the end of the novel, all of the important characters have revealed that they are not really what they seemed to be. Campbell, Resi Noth, George Kraft, Arpad Kovaks, even Campbell's closest friend during the war, Heinz Schildknecht, are all spies who assume false identities that are convincing enough to escape detection. All of them eventually become the roles they play. Kraft pretends to be a retired widower who paints to fill the empty hours, and he ends his life as a retired spy, happier in prison with his painting than at home in Russia with his wife. Resi Noth studies Campbell's plays so that she can play the role of Helga, and she ends her life like a heroine in one of his plays. Campbell insists that he is not really a Nazi and laments the fact that only three people knew his true identity as a spy, but Wirtanen reminds him that everyone who listened to his broadcasts "knew you for what you were, too" (187). All of these stories point to the moral that Vonnegut announces in his introduction: "We are what we pretend to be, so we must be careful what we pretend to be" (v). Stating a moral is a convenient way to reduce the theme of a novel to its essence, but the brevity and simplicity of a moral fails to capture the tensions and contradictions that make a theme interesting. In *Mother Night*, the tension between Campbell's ideal self and the role that he plays rips him apart. The process is painful to watch, excruciating to live through, but ultimately instructive. *Mother Night* reveals this tension to be at the center of the question of personal identity.

A CULTURAL POETICS READING

Developed in the 1970s and 1980s, cultural poetics is a critical approach that attempts to read texts in their historical and cultural contexts. Like any text, *Mother Night* is a product of the time period and culture in which it was written, but its many references to contemporary events make it an especially good candidate for a cultural poetics reading (for an introduction to cultural poetics, see chapter 3). In order to arrive at a reading of a text, a cultural poetics critic attempts to answer three basic questions: How are the author's experiences and beliefs reflected in the text? What are the rules and expectations of the culture in which the text was produced? How does the text add to the ongoing conversation about those rules?

Mother Night is the first of Vonnegut's novels to deal with World War II, so it is important to consider his experiences during the war to help us interpret the novel. Vonnegut describes himself as a pacifist, someone who is opposed to war, and his editorials for the Cornell student newspaper in the early 1940s argued against American involvement in World War II. However, when the United States entered the war, Vonnegut enlisted in the army and was sent to Europe. He was captured by German soldiers who noticed his German name and asked him why he was fighting "against [his] brothers" (Allen, *Conversations* 172). Vonnegut found this remark puzzling because he did not consider himself German. After World War I, many German Americans, including Vonnegut's parents, suppressed their cultural heritage as a way of proving their loyalty to the United States. This is important to keep in mind because one might assume that, as a German American, Vonnegut felt that his loyalty was divided between the two nations, like his protagonist, Howard W. Campbell, Jr. While he has repeatedly denied that he felt any personal attachment to Germany or its people, Vonnegut had to imagine what it would have been like to be a German during the war in order to create compelling fiction. In the novel's introduction, he admits that he probably "would have been a Nazi, bopping Jews and gypsies and Poles around, . . . warming myself with my secretly virtuous insides" (vii–viii). Such an admission requires an equal measure of courage and honesty, but without these qualities, no one can hope to understand how people can commit terrible atrocities and still think of themselves as virtuous.

As a prisoner of war, Vonnegut was taken to Dresden and put to work in a factory making malt syrup as a vitamin supplement for pregnant women. On February 13, 1945, the Allies dropped incendiary bombs on the city, creating a firestorm that killed 135,000 Germans, most of them civilians. Vonnegut and a few fellow prisoners survived because they were in a meat locker deep underground. After the bombing they were put to work as "corpse miners," breaking into cellars to remove bodies so they could be burned in massive funeral pyres to prevent an outbreak of disease. Such gruesome work confirmed Vonnegut's pacifism and led him to conclude that war, and the unquestioning nationalism that encourages it, are the real enemies of humankind.

This belief placed Vonnegut at odds with the majority of Americans in the late 1950s and early 1960s when he was writing *Mother Night*. American culture encouraged nationalism, although "patriotism," with its echoes of the American Revolution, was the preferred term. The cold war against the Soviet Union gave Americans an enemy to hate, just as they had been encouraged to hate the Germans during both world wars. The threat of nuclear annihilation prevented the cold war from heating up, but a wartime mentality of tension and paranoia prevailed. The United States and the Soviet Union spied on one another, and on April 31, 1960, the Soviets shot down a U2 spy plane over their territory and placed the pilot, Gary Powers, on trial. The cold war and the U2 incident made espionage a major national concern while Vonnegut was writing his novel about an American spy in Nazi Germany. Although the differences between Powers and Campbell are obvious, Powers's capture and trial became a major propaganda victory for the Soviets, the same kind of victory that Soviet agent Potapov attempts to engineer in *Mother Night*. In 1960, several prominent people suggested that Powers should have killed himself rather than allow the Soviets to capture him. Professor Robert Hutchins asked, "What [has] happened to great patriots like Nathan Hale?" (Halberstam 712). Hale's final words, "I only regret that I have but one life to lose for my country" were a rallying cry during the Revolutionary War, and Powers's failure to kill himself for the good of his country was considered symptomatic of a serious decline in American patriotism. Vonnegut expresses his disdain for this attitude in *Mother Night*. When the newspapers learn that Campbell is living in New York, one suggests that his "biggest war crime was not killing [himself] like a gentleman" to save the United States from embarrassment (162). Campbell replies that according to this logic, "Presumably Hitler was a gentleman" because he killed himself at the end of the war. *Mother Night* rejects the idea that it is honorable to value the interests of a nation above those of the individual. Frank Wirtanen often acts as Campbell's conscience by pointing out that his status as a spy does not absolve him from the guilt of also being a Nazi. Wirtanen earns his alias "Frank" by being frank with Campbell about the consequences of being a spy, and he always treats him fairly. At the end of the novel, Wirtanen commits treason against the U.S. government by corroborating Campbell's claim that he was a spy because he refuses to allow Campbell to be persecuted "by the forces of self-righteous nationalism" (267). In doing so, he places Campbell's interests ahead of those of his nation, indicating that our allegiance to our fellow human beings is more important than our duty to our country.

While Vonnegut was writing *Mother Night*, Adolph Eichmann, an S.S. officer who rounded up millions of Jews and sent them to the death camps, was captured by Israeli agents in Argentina and brought to Israel for trial. Eichmann appears briefly as a character in *Mother Night*, and the entire novel may be read as Vonnegut's response to the issues raised by his trial. Before his capture, Eichmann was interviewed by a journalist, and his memoirs were published in two installments in *Life* magazine in November 1960. Eichmann freely admitted to apprehending Jews and arranging for their transportation to the camps, but he claimed that this did not make him a "mass murderer." He portrayed himself as a "man of average character, with good qualities and many faults" (19). In the newspapers, Eichmann was often referred to as a "monster" (e.g., *New York Times*, 24 May 1960: 18). The crimes that he and other Nazis were accused of were so horrible that many writers found it difficult to think of them as human beings. More thoughtful commentators, including

Vonnegut and Telford Taylor, who was chief counsel at the Nuremberg
trials of Nazi war criminals, saw that the real question was how ordinary
people allowed themselves to commit such atrocities. In a review of William L. Shirer's *The Rise and Fall of the Third Reich: A History of Nazi
Germany*, Taylor pointed out that "the great horror of the Third Reich is
not that it was a government of monsters, but that it was a monstrous
government of—with relatively few exceptions—ordinary human beings" (*Saturday Review*, 15 Oct 1960: 23–24). Vonnegut's novel refuses to
allow readers to dismiss the Nazis as monsters and forces them to confront their own potential for evil.

Eichmann's trial and the publication of Shirer's acclaimed history of
Nazi Germany provided an opportunity for a re-evaluation of World
War II in 1960. It was a good time to pose the question What has the
world learned from the horrors of that time? Vonnegut's novel *Mother
Night* provides an accurate, if disappointing, answer: not much. Self-
righteous nationalism prevailed in the United States and the Soviet
Union, just as it had in Nazi Germany, and it led to an unprecedented
arms build up on both sides. Even the threat of nuclear annihilation was
not enough to force world leaders to compromise their nationalistic am-
bitions. Eichmann pointed out that not one Allied soldier was put on
trial for obeying orders that resulted in the death of civilians (*Life*, 28
Nov 1960: 19). While this certainly does nothing to diminish his guilt, it
does raise an important issue that was brushed aside at the time. Vonnegut hints at the unfairness of the one-sided justice that was dispensed
after the war by describing the firebombing of Dresden, but as he noted
in an interview, he hesitated to make the point more forcefully lest he
be seen as an apologist for the Nazis (Allen, *Conversations* 176). His
German ancestry made him even more cautious than he might have been
otherwise, but a careful reading of *Mother Night* reveals it to be a scathing
indictment of the nationalistic attitudes that make war into a righteous
crusade against evil, rather than a senseless slaughter of innocents. In
1960, few Americans were ready to listen to this message, and *Mother
Night* received little attention, but by considering the book in the cultural
context of the time, we can better appreciate the courage it took to write
it.

Cat's Cradle
(1963)

Kurt Vonnegut was an obscure writer when his fourth novel, *Cat's Cradle*, was published. The modest success of his first novel, which had appeared more than a decade earlier, had been forgotten. His two previous novels had appeared as paperback originals, so they had not been reviewed. Even though *Cat's Cradle* was published in hardcover, it seemed at first that it too would attract little attention. Only one review was published in the United States, a brief but positive notice in the *New York Times* by Terry Southern. In spite of these obstacles, *Cat's Cradle* found an audience and transformed Vonnegut from an obscure writer into a cult figure. Although most Americans were still not familiar with Vonnegut's work in the mid-1960s, he had a devoted group of fans who snapped up the paperback editions of his novels.

Vonnegut's surprising imagination is on full display in *Cat's Cradle*. This apocalyptic novel presents readers with a vision of the end of the world that is quite different from the nuclear annihilation that was widely feared in the 1960s. Vonnegut's world does not come to an end in a fiery bang; rather, the end is like the "great door of heaven being closed softly" (261). To a world obsessed with the destructive fire of the atom bomb, Vonnegut brings a vision of the world locked up in ice that will not melt. *Cat's Cradle* warns readers that science can devise many ways of ending the world, but it shows that human ingenuity can also make life worth living for the millions of human beings who currently live in poverty and despair. In *Cat's Cradle*, Vonnegut creates a new religion with a full set of scriptures and rituals, and he shows how it brings a sense of meaning and purpose to the lives of people who have found no consolation in other religions. He invents strange names—*karass, granfalloon*—for things we have known all our lives but never really thought about. By imagining another way that the world could end, he encourages readers to imagine new ways for life to continue.

PLOT DEVELOPMENT

Cat's Cradle begins with John, the first-person narrator, asking the reader to call him Jonah because, like the biblical Jonah, "somebody or something" has forced him to move from one place to another and to witness some pretty bizarre events. The opening page warns readers to expect strange coincidences and plot twists, and the rest of the novel does not disappoint. John is a freelance writer working on a book about what famous people were doing on the day that the atomic bomb was dropped on Hiroshima. *Cat's Cradle* tells the story of John's failed attempt to write this book and of his discovery of a new religion, "Bokononism," that provides him with a unique perspective on his own life and human history in general. As a Bokononist he looks back at his previous life as a nominal Christian with ironic detachment.

John's quest for information about what the "father" of the atomic bomb was doing on August 6, 1945, introduces him to the three children of Dr. Felix Hoenikker, Angela, Franklin, and Newton. Newton Hoenikker, better known as Newt, is a freshman who has just flunked out of Cornell University. Although he was only six years old when the bomb was dropped, he has vivid memories of that day because it was the only time his father ever tried to play with him. In a letter to John, Newt describes how Dr. Hoenikker became fascinated by a loop of string, fashioned it into a cat's cradle, and thrust it into his face, asking him to admire it. But Newt was more impressed by the ugliness of his father's face so close to his own, and he ran out of the house.

John makes no further progress on his book until about a year later when another assignment brings him to Ilium, New York, home of the General Forge and Foundry Company, where Dr. Hoenikker worked most of his life. Although the Hoenikker children no longer live there, John meets several people who knew them in high school and who describe them as social misfits. John tours the General Forge and Foundry research lab with Dr. Asa Breed, who was Dr. Hoenikker's supervisor, at least on paper. Dr. Breed admits that no one could really supervise

Dr. Hoenikker because he was like "a force of nature" (21). He worked without regard for what other people considered important. On his tour of the lab, which is modeled after the General Electric lab in Schenectady, New York, where Vonnegut worked for four years, John becomes aware of the tremendous gap between the scientists and the young women who type the results of their research. The typists, like the public in general, are mystified by science. They consider it a form of magic, and the company's educational exhibits do nothing to dispel the air of mystery. John's visit coincides with the week before Christmas, and the typists, who are known collectively as the "Girl Pool," come to Dr. Breed's office to sing carols and receive chocolate bars. One line from "O Little Town of Bethlehem" seems especially appropriate in the research lab that gave the world the atomic bomb: "The hopes and fears of all the years are here with us tonight." While Dr. Breed sees science as humanity's best hope for peace and prosperity, John is aware of its destructive potential and the fears it evokes in many ordinary people.

In order to explain Dr. Hoenikker's peculiar way of thinking, Dr. Breed tells John the story of "ice-nine." One day a U.S. Marine general visited the lab looking for a simple solution to a problem the marines have wallowed in since their inception—mud. Dr. Hoenikker thought for a moment and proposed the idea of ice-nine, a solid form of water with a much higher melting point than conventional ice. A small chip of ice-nine would be able to "teach" water molecules how to arrange themselves so that they would be solid at room temperature. The problem is that once ice-nine is released into the world it will solidify not just one particular body of water but all the streams that feed it, and the rivers connected to these streams, and then the oceans, locking up all the world's water and putting an end to life on earth. Dr. Breed declares ice-nine to be impossible, but John reveals that it already exits. Just before he died, Dr. Hoenikker created a small amount of ice-nine with a melting point of 114.4 degrees Fahrenheit. He told only his three children about it, and after he died, they divided the compound among themselves.

After his visit to the lab, John goes to the Ilium cemetery to see the grave of Dr. Hoenikker. His attention is immediately drawn to an enormous monument marking the grave of Dr. Hoenikker's wife Emily, which was erected by her three children, complete with poems expressing their devotion to her. This touching tribute makes John's cab driver think of his own mother's grave and inspires him to look for a larger stone to mark it. He takes John to a gravestone salesroom where they see a beautiful marble angel that is over one hundred years old. Carved by the present owner's great-grandfather, the stone was ordered by a

German immigrant who went west to Indiana without paying for it. The name on the stone is the narrator's. As he looks back on the strange coincidence of finding his own name on the gravestone, he describes it as his first *vin-dit*—a Bokononist term for a strong push toward the belief that God is guiding the course of one's life. Looking at his own name on the stone, he has a vision of "tunnels" connecting all human beings throughout history and giving their lives meaning and direction.

While he was in Ilium, John let a poet named Sherman Krebbs stay in his apartment. When he returns he finds that Krebbs has wrecked the place, killed his cat and his avocado tree, burned his couch, and written a poem in excrement on the kitchen floor. Krebbs is a nihilist, someone who believes in nothing and finds life meaningless. John says he was tempted to see the coincidence of the stone angel as meaningless and to conclude that life itself was meaningless, but Krebbs's outlandish behavior convinces him that nihilism is a mistake. Krebbs gives him another shove in the direction of Bokononism, which argues that everything happens for a reason, even if the reason is not immediately apparent.

A series of strange coincidences propels John into contact with Frank Hoenikker, who disappeared shortly after his father's funeral. John sees an advertising supplement in the *New York Times* for the tiny island nation of San Lorenzo. On the cover is a picture of a breathtakingly beautiful woman, Mona Aamons Monzano, and John falls instantly in love (80). Looking inside for more pictures of Mona, he instead comes across Frank Hoenikker, who is San Lorenzo's "Minister of Science and Progress" (80). Then he is assigned to write an article on another resident of the island, Julian Castle, who gave up a life of wealth and privilege to found a hospital and care for San Lorenzo's poor. On the plane to San Lorenzo, he meets Horlick Minton, the new U.S. ambassador, and his wife Claire. The Mintons are devoted to each other and pay very little attention to anyone else. Having been dismissed briefly from the diplomatic service for expressing the opinion that Americans are not universally loved, they view their new assignment with cynical detachment. The Mintons show John a copy of a book on San Lorenzo by Philip Castle, the son of philanthropist Julian Castle. The book introduces John to the Bokononist religion and gives him a glimpse of the island's long, sad history. Bokonon, whose real name, Johnson, became "Bokonon" in the island's strange dialect, is a black man originally from Trinidad who traveled the world before his fate finally delivered him to San Lorenzo. Faced with the hopeless poverty of a large population on an island with few resources, Bokonon and his fellow traveler Earl McCabe created a religion called Bokononism and pitted it against a repressive government headed by McCabe. Bokonon used depression-era bodybuilder Charles Atlas's concept of "dynamic tension" as the basis for a system that turned life on the island into a morality play in which good and evil battle endlessly. Bokonon took on the role of the persecuted holy man hiding out in the jungle, while McCabe became the dictatorial president who punished all Bokononists with death on a giant fishhook. Although the new system did not improve the economic conditions on the island, it improved the lives of the people by making them actors in a cosmic drama and giving their lives meaning.

John also meets H. Lowe Crosby, a bicycle manufacturer who hopes to build a factory in San Lorenzo, and his wife Hazel. Like the narrator, Hazel is from Indiana, and she delights in meeting other "Hoosiers" and expounding on the great things that have been accomplished by people from Indiana. Hazel's mania for Hoosiers gives John an opportunity to introduce the Bokononist concepts of the *karass* and the *granfalloon*. A *karass* is a team that does "God's Will" without realizing it, while a *granfalloon* is a false *karass* composed of people who supposedly have something in common, but which has nothing to do with God's plans. Crosby is attracted to San Lorenzo because the people are poor and supposedly desperate for any opportunity to earn a living, so he expects they will work hard and not give him any trouble, unlike the unionized workers back home. "Papa" Monzano, McCabe's successor as the island's dictatorial president-for-life, punishes any kind of crime by hoisting the perpetrator on a large fish hook and letting him hang in public until he dies. While Crosby admits that this may be too brutal for a democracy, he does favor the reinstatement of public hanging to restore a healthy respect for the law in the United States. Crosby is the novel's spokesman for American capitalism. He claims to love democracy and freedom but actually prefers a dictatorship that promises him total power over his workers.

The plane trip also gives John time to get to know two of Dr. Hoenikker's children, thirty-four-year-old Angela and nineteen-year-old Newt, who are flying to San Lorenzo to attend their brother Frank's wedding. Frank is engaged to Mona Aamons Monzano, which is disappointing news for John, who claims to have fallen in love with her picture in the *New York Times*.

When the plane arrives in San Lorenzo, it is greeted by 5,000 of the island's listless inhabitants, a marching band that does not play, and a seriously ill president who collapses in the middle of his welcoming speech. After Papa Monzano is whisked away to his mountain top castle in an ambulance, the Mintons are taken to the U.S. embassy, Angela and

Newt accompany Frank to his home, and John and the Crosbys are taken
to Casa Mona, a gleaming new hotel in Bolivar, the capital city. Soon
after his arrival at the hotel, John receives a call from Frank asking him
to come to his house for dinner. There he meets Julian Castle, the philanthropist he is supposed to interview. John is shocked to learn that the
saintly Castle, founder of the House of Hope and Mercy in the jungle,
is actually a sneering nihilist who believes that all human beings are
"vile" (169). Castle fills John in on some details of the island's history
while they wait for Frank to arrive. Although Bokononism is outlawed
and punishable by death, everyone on the island, including Papa Monzano, is a Bokononist. The persecution of Bokononism is an elaborate
game, meant to give the religion more "zest" (173). With Papa Monzano
on his deathbed, Frank is next in line to assume the presidency of San
Lorenzo. However, like his father, Frank is not comfortable with people,
and he prefers to work behind the scenes. He offers John the presidency.
When he recovers from the shock, John agrees, explaining his decision
in Bokononist terms as giving in to what he feels is his destiny. John
then learns that *The Books of Bokonon* predict that Mona will marry the
next president of San Lorenzo, and it appears that the fantasy that began
when he saw her picture in the paper will soon come true. Together they
perform the Bokononist ceremony of *boko-maru*, placing the soles of their
feet together so that their souls may also touch. Immediately afterward,
John ruins this special moment by insisting that Mona reserve all her
love for him. She counters that she loves everyone equally, as her religion
requires. For a Bokononist, demanding all of someone's love is the
greatest sin. Faced with losing Mona, John decides to become a Bokononist, marry Mona, and become president of San Lorenzo.

Frank decides that it would be a good idea to get Papa Monzano's
blessing for this plan, so they travel to his evil-looking black castle
perched on a precipice high above the sea. Monzano is on his deathbed,
which happens to be the gilded dinghy that brought Bokonon to San
Lorenzo so many years before. He approves of John becoming the next
president and tells him to kill Bokonon and teach the people science
because "science is magic that *works*" (218). A ceremony is scheduled for
later that day to commemorate the deaths of the "Hundred Martyrs to
Democracy," young San Lorenzans who died on their way to fight in
World War II (233). Frank plans to announce John's presidency at the
same ceremony. Unable to bear the pain of the cancer that is killing him
slowly, Papa Monzano eats a crystal of ice-nine that Frank has given him
and dies instantly, frozen solid. Not realizing what killed Monzano, his
doctor dies after touching him, and when his frozen body falls, he scat-

ters chunks of ice-nine all over the floor of the bedroom. Frank, Angela, Newt, and John begin a frantic cleanup and plan to dispose of the bodies in a massive funeral pyre. But before they can finish their work, one of the airplanes saluting the hundred martyrs crashes into the side of the castle, sending Monzano's frozen body into the sea, which immediately freezes along with most of the water on earth.

Almost immediately, huge tornadoes fill the skies and scatter the survivors of the castle's collapse. John and Mona find refuge in an air-raid shelter that Monzano had stocked with food and water in anticipation of nuclear war. After a week underground, they surface to find an almost totally lifeless world. Although the killer tornadoes have retreated, death is everywhere in the frost-like crystals of ice-nine. As Mona points out, "Mother Earth isn't a very good mother anymore" (269). After wandering about aimlessly, John and Mona stumble upon the scene of a mass suicide. Gathered together in a round valley are thousands of frozen San Lorenzans. In the center of this group, under a rock, John finds a note from Bokonon explaining that the ice-nine statues in the valley are most of the survivors of the tornadoes that came in the wake of the freezing of the ocean. They found Bokonon and demanded that he explain why God had done this and tell them what to do now. He told them that God must be trying to kill them and that they should succumb to his will and die by eating ice-nine. John is appalled by Bokonon's cynicism, but Mona finds it amusing, and she recalls that Bokonon always said he would never follow his own advice "because he knew it was worthless" (273). She asks John if he really wishes that these people were alive again, and he cannot answer her. Then she bends down, pulls up a crystal of the ice-nine, touches it to her lips, and becomes a statue like the rest of her compatriots.

John soon finds the other survivors of the apocalypse, Frank, Newt, and the Crosbys, living like the "Swiss Family Robinson" in the ruin of Frank's house (276). Although no animals or plants have survived, ice-nine preserves pigs, goats, and chickens until the survivors are ready to thaw and eat them. They live this way for six months while John writes his book, Hazel sews an American flag, Newt paints, Crosby cooks, and Franks studies an ant farm. As far as they know, ants are the only other form of life to survive.

On a trip to Bolivar to get more paint for Newt, John finally meets Bokonon, who is sitting by the side of the road writing the final lines of his book. John has been searching for an appropriately symbolic way to end his own life, and the quote from Bokonon that ends the novel apparently gives it to him. Bokonon says that, were he a younger man, he would write "a history of human stupidity," take it to the top of Mount McCabe, place it under his head, and make himself into an ice-nine statue, thumbing his nose at God (287).

CHARACTER DEVELOPMENT

Cat's Cradle contains several of Vonnegut's most memorable characters, including the narrator John or "Jonah," Dr. Felix Hoenikker and his children, and Julian Castle. John, the narrator-protagonist, is clearly the most important character in the novel, and yet we are given few biographical details about him. He is a freelance writer who adopts a cynical attitude toward life, even as he searches for something to believe in. He has been twice married and divorced, and his second wife left him because he is "too pessimistic" (77). Unlike most of the other characters, he is concerned with the human consequences of science and technology. He takes grim pleasure in pointing out the ironies that other characters cannot see. For instance when Angela complains that her father was never adequately compensated for all his marvelous inventions, John contrasts her selfish lament with the grinding poverty that San Lorenzans endure in silence. He takes some pride in being a man of the world, but even that pride is tinged with irony. He confesses to Mona that he also considers himself the "world's champion mistake maker" (204). His cynicism is meant to hide deep insecurities, but it often cracks, leaving him open and vulnerable. Although he calls Hazel Crosby a "barn-yard fool," he finds "deep, idiotic relief" in her motherly embrace after the death of Mona (274). In spite of his pessimism, he dreams of a better world. As he thinks about what he will do as president of San Lorenzo, he indulges in utopian fantasies of peace and prosperity for all people. Even after the ice-nine apocalypse, he keeps turning the conversation to what might have been if people had only managed science and nature more wisely.

Although Dr. Felix Hoenikker is dead before the present action of the novel begins, he is still a major character. His first name, "Felix," is both appropriate and ironic. Felix means "happy," and Hoenikker certainly is happy as he enjoys an endless childhood of discovery and wonder, but his happiness is paid for by a vast amount of human misery. John's search for information about him gets the story going, and throughout the novel, John learns more and more about the strange man who gave the world the atom bomb and ice-nine. The most common view of Hoenikker is that he is the scientific equivalent of a saint because he does not care about money or fame, only about discovering the truth. In his brief speech accepting the Nobel Prize, he states that his accomplishments are due to the fact that he retains the curiosity of an eight year old. Unfortunately for humanity, he is childlike in other ways as well. He has no sense of moral responsibility for how his discoveries might be used. When a fellow scientist tries to point out that the atom bomb is sinful, Hoenikker replies, "What is sin?" (17). He also evades his responsibilities as a husband and a father, leaving his wife bereft of love and companionship and turning his children into emotional cripples. Although many of his actions are amusing on the surface, such as leaving a tip for his wife after she has served him breakfast, they reveal a spiritual emptiness and a total lack of concern for others that has dire consequences for the entire planet.

Dr. Hoenikker's three children all suffer from his failure as a father. Each one has a physical disability that is only the outward sign of a more significant psychic wound. None of them has the emotional maturity to resist the temptation to use ice-nine to buy a little love and acceptance. Angela, the eldest, is a "horse-faced" giant who hunches over in a desperate attempt to minimize her height (111). When her mother died giving birth to Newt, Angela became a mother to her younger siblings and to her childish father, who in spite of his genius is incapable of caring for himself. She withdrew from high school and devoted herself to the family, depriving herself of friendship and love in the process. Her only creative outlet is the clarinet, which she plays as if possessed by a demon. Her lack of experience with men led her to a loveless marriage to an arms manufacturer who was looking for the secret of ice-nine. Like her father, she is incapable of realizing how her actions will affect others. She treats her brother Newt as if he was still a child, without considering how this makes him feel.

Newt, the youngest of the Hoenikker children, is a midget. In spite of the obvious difficulty of being a very small man in a culture that values men for their size and strength, Newt is the most mature and well-adjusted member of the Hoenikker family. His small stature makes him look like a child and symbolizes the lasting effect of his father's failure to assume adult responsibilities. Without a role model, the Hoenikker children remain children all their lives. Newt is obsessed with the memory of his father thrusting a cat's cradle in his face when he was six years old. He cannot get past the disappointment of finding neither cat nor cradle in the string figure. For Newt, the meaningless tangle of string becomes a symbol of the lack of meaning in human life. Newt's persistent childishness makes it easy for a Russian spy named Zinka to steal ice-nine by pretending that she is in love with him. Yet, in an ironic twist, Newt's small size helps him to achieve a level of maturity that his siblings never match. The narrator points out that he is "shrewdly watchful" of his larger companions. He submits to Angela's insensitive and persistent mothering with an "amiable grace" (111). Furthermore, he seems to have achieved a measure of peace through his painting. He does not care what others think of the finished product, but after completing a dark image of the cat's cradle that haunts his memory, he falls asleep. As the novel ends, Newt is scavenging for more paint in the ruins of San Lorenzo, suggesting that his art gives him a way to cope with even the most desperate situations.

Franklin "Frank" Hoenikker is described as a "fox-faced, immature young man," and a "pinch-faced child," even though he is twenty-six at the time (80, 194). From an early age, Frank craves power over living things. One of his favorite youthful pastimes is putting bugs in a jar and making them fight by shaking the jar. When asked what he is doing, he replies "experimenting," suggesting that he wants to identify with his father's attempts to understand and control the physical world. As a high school student, he creates a miniature town in the basement of a local model shop. His attention to detail is so obsessive that every tiny doorknob on every tiny house really works. Creating this little world gives Frank a chance to play God on a small scale, just as his father is playing God by creating weapons that can destroy life on earth. Frank rises to power on San Lorenzo by giving its ruthless and irresponsible dictator a piece of ice-nine, a decision that ultimately results in the end of almost all life. One might expect that such a blunder would be ample cause for remorse, but Frank is no more concerned with the consequences of his actions than his father was. After the apocalypse, he spends his time observing an ant farm and consoling himself with the obviously mistaken notion that he had "grown up a good deal" (218).

Mona Aamons Monzano is more a symbol than a character, and perhaps this accounts for her apparent lack of human feeling. We are told that because she is the only beautiful woman on San Lorenzo, she is a "national erotic symbol" (120). For John, she represents "peace and plenty forever," the fulfillment of all his erotic fantasies (140). He describes her as if she were a perfect classical statue, foreshadowing her death when she becomes an ice-nine statue. She claims to love everyone equally, and she seems indifferent to whatever may happen to her. She is unmoved when she discovers the frozen bodies of thousands San Lorenzans, and she laughs as she becomes a statue herself. The name Mona calls to mind the famous painting the "Mona Lisa" and provides an important clue to her role in the novel. She represents the perfection of art: beauty itself, unattainable, eternal, serene. Attempting to summarize his first impression of Mona, John echoes the final lines of Keats' "Ode on a Grecian Urn":

"Beauty is truth, truth beauty,"—that is all
Ye know on earth, and all ye need to know.

He says that Mona "seemed to understand all, and to be all there was to understand" (140).

Julian Castle is a vividly drawn minor character who underscores two of the novel's major themes: personal responsibility and the search for meaning in life. As the heir to an enormous sugar fortune, Castle wasted the first forty years of his life in an irresponsible search for pleasure, reminiscent of the early days of Malachi Constant in *The Sirens of Titan*. Then, in an abrupt change of direction, he founded a free hospital in San Lorenzo and dedicated the next twenty years of his life to serving the poor. Like Dr. Hoenikker, he is widely regarded as a saint, but by the time readers meet Castle, Hoenikker's example has made them wary of accepting that term at face value. Sure enough, Castle is anything but saintly in his mannerisms and opinions. He talks out of the corner of his mouth like a movie gangster, sneers at his own good works, and punctuates his "satanic" remarks by jabbing at his listeners with a big cigar (169). One moment he claims to be a devoted follower of Jesus Christ, and the next he shrugs it off as a meaningless remark that reflects the meaninglessness of everything. Like Sherman Krebbs, Castle is a nihilist, but unlike Krebbs he has decided to devote himself to caring for his fellow human beings in spite of his belief that "man is vile, and man makes nothing worth making, knows nothing worth knowing" (169). Krebbs uses his nihilism as an excuse for his failure to take responsibility for his selfish actions, but Castle's nihilism inspires him to assume responsibility, not only for himself, but also for San Lorenzo's poor. His devotion remains constant to the end, and he dies trying to reach his hospital amid the tornadoes that herald the end of the world. If we grant that it is possible to be a saint without faith in God, then Castle is a saint.

THEMATIC ISSUES

One of the major themes of *Cat's Cradle* is announced even before the novel begins. Between the dedication page and the table of contents are two epigraphs that sum up the dynamic relationship between truth and falsehood that the novel explores. The first epigraph announces that "nothing in this book is true." In one sense, this is a crude summary of the standard disclaimer that appears on the copyright page of this novel and most others, declaring the book to be a work of fiction and claiming that any resemblance between characters in the novel and real people is coincidental. Vonnegut parodied the standard disclaimer in *The Sirens of Titan* by claiming that everything in that fantastic novel was true in order to suggest the complex relationship between fiction and truth (see chapter 4 of this volume). The second epigraph is credited to *The Books of Bokonon*, a meaningless reference to those who have not already read the novel. "Live by the *foma* [harmless untruths] that make you brave and kind and healthy and happy." These contradictory statements force readers to wonder what Vonnegut means by "truth" and put them in the proper frame of mind to appreciate the novel that follows.

One possible meaning of "true" is consistent with the facts of real life. In this sense, the novel is obviously not true because the island of San Lorenzo does not exist and water does not freeze at 114 degrees Fahrenheit. Dr. Hoenikker spent his life in the pursuit of his kind of truth, but the novel suggests repeatedly that mere facts about how the world works are not enough to satisfy most human beings. After the ice-nine apocalypse, John treats Mona to "one of the secrets of life" that scientists spent years discovering: "Animals breathe in what animals breathe out, and vice versa" (268). Of course, this should read: Animals breathe in what plants breathe out and vice-versa. Whether this error was intentional on Vonnegut's part or a lapse in proofreading, it underscores the essential triviality of scientific truth. The mechanisms of animal and plant respiration, known to scientists as the Krebbs cycle, are essential to life on earth and worthy subjects of study, but when someone promises to reveal "one of the secrets of life," most people hope for more than a lecture, especially in a novel where Krebbs is also the name of a cat-murdering nihilist. Human beings crave a higher form of truth that will give meaning to their daily lives. Religions have supplied these higher truths in the past, but in part because of advances in science, spiritual truths have become suspect in the twentieth century. Bokonon realizes that all religions are founded on lies, but he also realizes that people need good, helpful lies if they are to cope successfully with their lives. He emphasizes his religion's usefulness rather than its truthfulness and constantly reminds his followers that he is telling them lies. While most religions encourage their adherents to believe in the truth of the stories they tell, Bokonon considers belief dangerous. When people believe that they have the "Truth," they seek to impose their beliefs on others, and religious wars are the inevitable result. The highest truth in Bokonon's religion is that all spiritual truths are actually useful fictions, creations of the imagination that do not exist outside of the human mind. The meaning of life is not something we can discover in the outside world. We must create it for ourselves.

Picking up on a theme that Vonnegut introduced in *Player Piano*, *Cat's Cradle* points out that science became a kind of false religion that filled a spiritual vacuum in the twentieth century. Dr Hoenikker is repeatedly called a "saint," and Dr. Breed describes the advancement of scientific knowledge as a holy quest that will lead to paradise on earth. Important events in the novel, including John's visit to the research lab and Dr. Hoenikker's death, coincide with Christmas, and Christian symbols intertwine with scientific apparatus to suggest the birth of a new religion. Like priests of the Middle Ages, scientists possess secret knowledge that mystifies the common people. Although they claim that their knowledge is the opposite of magic, to the uninitiated masses it is just as incomprehensible, powerful, and fearsome. Dr. Hoenikker is described as a "Christmas elf" who bestows his "last gift" to humanity, ice-nine, on Christmas Eve (114, 50). The parallels with Christianity highlight the spiritual emptiness of scientific research conducted in a moral vacuum, without appropriate consideration of the human consequences of scientific discovery. In spite of these harsh criticisms of science-as-religion, it would be inaccurate to argue that *Cat's Cradle* has an antiscience theme. The joy that Hoenikker feels in the process of discovery and the childlike sense of wonder that he maintains throughout his life are celebrated as true achievements, even as his failure to assume responsibility for his discoveries is condemned.

Joy and childlike wonder are also essential to the creation of art, and the role that art can play in the search for meaning in human life is another important theme in the novel. Newt achieves peace and a sense of purpose through his painting, but the other characters' reactions to his work reveal an important distinction between the process of creating art and the final product. The narrator calls Newt's painting "dreadful," but it inspires him to write a pretty creative sentence as he attempts to describe it to his readers. He compares the scratches Newt has made on a black background to a spider's web, and then wonders if they might not represent "the sticky nets of human futility hung up on a moonless night to dry" (164). Of course, this is not what Newt had in mind, but it does not matter. What counts is the process of creating meaning, in paint or in words, not the final product.

Frank's fantastic house, which was designed and built by Mona's architect father, is another example of how art can give meaning to human life. It straddles a waterfall and seems to grow out of the natural environment, but its primary effect is "to announce that a man had been whimsically busy there" (163). As the son and grandson of architects, Vonnegut realizes that architecture is an art that is also a science. An architect strives to design a house that is beautiful and functional but needs scientific knowledge so that it will not fall down. Art and science merge harmoniously in Frank's house, and the novel suggests that to be "whimsically busy" is the highest form of happiness that humans can hope for in life. Bokonon founded his religion on this concept and alleviated the unhappiness of the people of San Lorenzo by making them all actors in a "living legend," so that their everyday lives became a work of art in the making (174).

SYMBOLISM

Art achieves its effect by creating symbols, and *Cat's Cradle* is no exception. A close examination of the novel's central symbols will reveal its intricate architecture. The most obvious and important symbol is the cat's cradle that gives the novel its title. To make a cat's cradle, one must first tie the ends of a piece of string together to form an endless loop. The novel itself has a circular structure because readers cannot appreciate the full significance of the epigraphs until they have finished reading and returned to the beginning. Circles are used to symbolize nothing, as in the figure for zero [0], and everything, as in the symbol for infinity, a loop that crosses itself. Circles traditionally symbolize wholeness, because the line has no end, and emptiness, because the area inside is empty. But a loop of string is not a cat's cradle until human hands shape it, so the cat's cradle becomes a symbol of our ability to shape the world around us and by shaping it, give it meaning. Newt Hoenikker, who as an adult is still terrified by the memory of his father thrusting a cat's cradle in his face, has done some research on the game. He points out that humans have been making cat's cradles for hundreds of thousands of years, and the activity is part of cultures all over the world. The long history and universality of the cat's cradle makes it a perfect symbol for all of humanity's varied attempts to structure the world in a meaningful way, including magic, religion, fiction, philosophy, and science. For Newt, the cat's cradle represents parental tyranny over children because it figures so prominently in his own childhood trauma: "No wonder kids grow up crazy. A cat's cradle is nothing but a bunch of X's between somebody's hands. . . . *No damn cat and no damn cradle.*" Some readers assume that Newt's opinion is authoritative because he is the novel's resident expert on cat's cradles, but the rest of the novel suggests deeper meanings for the symbol. On the literal level, Newt is correct; there really is neither cat nor cradle in a cat's cradle. But the novel insists repeatedly that human creations are not to be taken literally but should be seen as creative fictions. The point of making a cat's cradle is not to create a real cat and a real cradle, but to have fun making something out of nothing. In fact, the cat's cradle is only one of the many figures that can be made from a loop of string. The joy of the game comes from transforming one figure into another, and it is comparable to the joy that Bokonon felt in transforming elements of Christianity into his new religion. As Bokonon repeatedly warns, the harm arises only when we begin to think of our fanciful figures as literally true—when we expect a real cat and a real cradle.

Vonnegut engages in a similar sort of transformational play through-out the novel, and the symbol of the cat's cradle appears in many different guises. When Jack, the owner of the hobby shop, tells John about his attempt to restore order to his life after his wife has left him, he uses the image of a cat's cradle: "I'm still trying to pull the strings of my life back together" (74). In this way, a chance remark by a minor character becomes part of the symbolic web that gives the novel its distinctive shape. Probably the most significant transformation of the cat's cradle symbol can be found in Vonnegut's description of the fanciful house designed by Nestor Aamons, Mona's father. We have already seen that it represents a marriage of art and science through creative play, but it is also a sort of cat's cradle, "a cunning lattice of very light steel posts and beams" (163). In engineering terms, the purpose of the lattice is to distribute the weight of the terrace so that it can be borne by light steel beams that could never support it otherwise. The architect achieves structural strength and stability by creating "dynamic tension," between the posts and beams, just as Bokonon framed a new social order for San Lorenzo by creating dynamic tension between groups of people (120). Like the lattice design, Bokonon's new religion reduces the burden of human existence by distributing it more evenly. Obviously creating a perfect society on a desperately poor island is more difficult than de-signing an artful house. Human beings are not as strong and reliable as steel beams. As Julian Castle explains to John, both Bokonon and McCabe cracked under the weight of their roles and went insane, but the symbol of the cat's cradle allows Vonnegut to explore the underlying similarities between activities as diverse as art, science, religion, and sociology. The tension in the strings gives the cat's cradle its shape. The tension in the steel gives the lattice its strength. The tension in the novel between the opposed forces of nihilism and belief and art and science gives it symbolic power, not to resolve these conflicts in favor of one side or another, but to show that dynamic tension between them is essential to a creative and fulfilling life.

AN INTERTEXTUAL READING

An intertextual approach to reading a novel recognizes that all texts are part of a cultural web that links them to other texts. By examining the relationships between texts, we achieve a deeper understanding of individual texts and of the culture that produced them. An intertextual approach assumes that writers' visions of the world are shaped by their culture, which includes language, customs, beliefs, and, perhaps most importantly, other literary texts. Intertextual critics view literature as an ongoing conversation. Writers find their place in the conversation by commenting on, revising, critiquing, or parodying the work of earlier writers. Previous works of literature provide them with a storehouse of symbols that are familiar to readers and have accumulated power through repeated use.

The first sentence of *Cat's Cradle* invokes two well-known works of literature in only three words: "Call me Jonah" (1). The most obvious reference is to the book of Jonah in the Bible, in which God calls the prophet Jonah to travel to Nineveh and warn its citizens to give up their evil ways or he will destroy the city. Jonah does not want to go, so he gets on a ship bound in the opposite direction. A furious storm erupts, and the sailors try to determine who has brought the wrath of God upon them. Jonah confesses, they pitch him overboard, and he is swallowed by an enormous fish. After three days in the fish's belly, Jonah is cast up on shore, and he decides to go to Nineveh and preach as the Lord demanded. The people of Nineveh repent and the city is saved, but rather than being pleased by the effectiveness of his preaching, Jonah is mad at God for not following through on his promise to destroy Nineveh. God replies that he is more concerned with the lives of Nineveh's people than with making Jonah's prophecy come true.

In the popular imagination, Jonah has become synonymous with bad luck, but Vonnegut's narrator says that is not why he wants to be called Jonah. Instead, he uses the name because "somebody or something has compelled me to be certain places at certain times" (1). In the biblical story there is no doubt about who controls human destiny. God speaks directly to Jonah, reveals his plans, and then explains why he changed them. In *Cat's Cradle*, there is no such certainty. Some characters are nihilists, denying the existence of God and arguing that human life is meaningless. Others are Bokononists, who believe that everything happens for a reason and contributes to the fulfillment of God's plan. Unlike Jonah, John must sift through subtle clues in an attempt to make sense of why so many strange things happen to him, and he has no assurance that the conclusions he reaches have any validity. Invoking the biblical story allows Vonnegut to highlight the fundamental uncertainty of contemporary life.

Jonah could be described as a reluctant prophet of doom, and the same phrase applies to John. He plans to call his book about Hiroshima *The Day The World Ended*. The title is not literally true, but it does suggest that he plans to present Hiroshima as a portent of nuclear apocalypse. *Cat's Cradle*, the book he actually writes, is also a prophecy of what will happen if we allow scientists to create ever more efficient weapons of mass destruction. One reason Jonah is reluctant to preach to the people of Nineveh is that he fears they will ignore him. John shares Jonah's pessimism about the effectiveness of his preaching. He quotes Bokonon's ironic injunction to "write it all down" so that people can "avoid making serious mistakes in the future" (237). Reviewing human history, John can find no evidence that knowledge of past mistakes has ever helped people avoid making more. Besides, within the world of the novel, his writing has a very small audience, the few survivors on San Lorenzo, and it is too late to warn people about ice-nine. The final lines of the novel are a quote from the final chapter of the *Books of Bokonon*, and they suggest that John should climb Mt. McCabe with his manuscript, which is "a history of human stupidity," lie down with the book under his head, and make himself into an ice-nine statue, "grinning horribly, and thumbing my nose at You Know Who" (287). If John actually takes Bokonon's advice he will be following in the footsteps of Jonah, who defied God in spite of ample evidence of His power and mercy. But is John really a Jonah? Many readers have assumed that John will follow Bokonon's advice, but there are compelling reasons to suggest that he will not. Mona has already told John that Bokonon would never follow his own advice because he knows that it is "worthless" (273). Bokonon's final calypso, painted in the ruins of San Lorenzo's castle, points out the folly of scolding God: "He'll just smile and nod" (270). More importantly, the entire novel argues that humans must assume responsibility for their own destiny. Blaming the end of the human race on God is the ultimate evasion of that responsibility. Writing a "history of human stupidity," as Vonnegut has done in *Cat's Cradle*, and publishing it as a warning while there is still time for us to change direction is one way of assuming the prophet's responsibility that the biblical Jonah persistently tries to shirk.

One way to read the Book of Jonah is as a satire on prophets and prophecy (for a discussion of satire, see chapter 2 of this volume). Jonah is ridiculed for caring more about being right than about the people he was trying to save. *Cat's Cradle* is also a satire, but in the novel, the main targets are the "saints" of the new religion of science, who pursue abstract truth without considering its human consequences. Just as the Book of Jonah points out the discrepancies between God's plans for Jonah and his cowardly and selfish actions, so *Cat's Cradle* demonstrates the gap between the stated mission of science, to improve human life, and its actual products, which include weapons of mass destruction.

The novel's opening sentence also calls to mind the first line of Herman Melville's novel, *Moby Dick*: "Call me Ishmael." In both novels, the request raises questions about the narrator's identity. Is that his real name? If not, why did he pick it? What is the relationship between names and the things they stand for? Both novels point out the limits of human knowledge and suggest how much lies outside of our understanding. In *Moby Dick*, the white whale that Captain Ahab pursues relentlessly symbolizes the incomprehensibility of nature. Ahab's desire to kill the whale represents humanity's quest to subdue nature, and the same quest is at that heart of *Cat's Cradle*. In *Moby Dick*, the unsuccessful attempt to kill the whale results in the destruction of the little world of the whaleship, but in *Cat's Cradle*, Dr. Hoenikker's success in creating ice-nine leads to the destruction of almost all life on earth. Although Hoenikker apparently succeeds in controlling nature, his creation turns on him, just as the white whale turns on Ahab and destroys his ship. In *Moby Dick*, Melville argues that the whiteness of the whale is what makes him so horrible. It is a reversal of the natural order that reminds human beings how small we are and how limited our understanding of the world is. Vonnegut takes this insight even further and invites his readers to contemplate the horror of an entire world turned white and lifeless: "The moist green earth was a blue-white pearl" (261).

An intertextual reading reveals that in a sense ice-nine is Vonnegut's white whale, but he also plays with the symbol in other ways. Mount McCabe, the tallest mountain on San Lorenzo, is described as "cetacean," whale-like, recalling Melville's chapter on cetology, the study of whales, in *Moby Dick*. John goes on to describe the mountain's "fearful hump" as a "blue whale." The peak of the mountain is a stone outcropping that resembles "the stump of a snapped harpoon," which should remove any doubt that Vonnegut had Melville in mind as he wrote this passage (210). Just as no one succeeded in killing Moby Dick, so no one has ever climbed Mount McCabe, but here the parallels end and Vonnegut introduces a significant difference that shows how his response to Moby Dick differs from the original. No one has climbed Mount McCabe because no one has bothered to try, not because it presents any real difficulties. Climbing a mountain and placing a flag there, as Hazel Crosby wants John to do, is a way of trying to conquer nature. To the Bokononists, this is a meaningless gesture that reveals a fundamental misunderstanding of the proper relationship between man and nature. Vonnegut taps into the symbolic power of the Book of Jonah and *Moby Dick* in order to warn his readers against trying to control forces that they can never understand.

7

God Bless You, Mr. Rosewater
(1965)

God Bless You, Mr. Rosewater returns to a question that is at the heart of Vonnegut's first novel, *Player Piano*: How can people build meaningful lives in a world where machines do most of the work? Unlike *Player Piano*, which is set in the future when machines have already replaced most humans, *Rosewater* is set in the America of the 1960s. Although labor-saving devices were just beginning to replace factory workers at this time, the novel points out that a feeling of uselessness was already starting to spread among the working class. *Rosewater* also takes on the idle rich by showing that their lives are just as useless as those who have lost their factory jobs. Indeed few segments of American society escape Vonnegut's satiric attacks. The novel castigates both liberals and conservatives, mocking the simplistic solutions of social reformers even as it chides those who refuse to help others.

God Bless You, Mr. Rosewater is even more relevant to today's society than it was in the 1960s. The gap between rich and poor has widened since the book was published. Relatively well-paying factory jobs have been replaced by poorly paid, demeaning work in the new "service economy." Conservative politicians continue to blame the victims of economic change and accuse them of being lazy. Vonnegut's satire on mean-spiritedness in all its forms is just as sharp today as it was in 1965.

PLOT DEVELOPMENT

God Bless You, Mr. Rosewater tells the story of Eliot Rosewater, heir to
a large fortune, war hero, philanthropist, alcoholic, and either the sanest,
or one of the craziest, men of his era. Norman Mushari, a lawyer who
works for the firm that set up the Rosewater Foundation, puts the novel's
plot in motion by scheming to take control of the foundation away from
Eliot and pass it to a distant cousin. A clause in the foundation's charter
says that its president may be removed only if he is proven insane. The
novel opens in 1964, and Mushari is examining his law firm's private
files on Eliot, looking for information that will convince a judge that Eliot
is crazy.

In terms of plot development, it is useful to divide the novel into two
sections: The first fifty-seven pages describe Mushari's investigation of
Eliot's past, while the rest of the book deals with Mushari's attempt to
transfer control of the foundation. Beginning the novel with Mushari's
investigation allows Vonnegut to summarize briefly the major events of
the first forty-six years of Eliot's life, to engage the reader's interest, and,
most importantly, to create an ironic point of view. The second section
of the book takes place during three days in June 1964 and a single day
in June of the following year.

By focusing on the investigation of Rosewater in the first section of
the novel rather than giving a direct account of Eliot's life, Vonnegut
adds a level of irony that functions like a frame for the novel's portrait
of Eliot Rosewater. Readers do not see Eliot through Mushari's eyes, as
they would if the story were told in the first person, but they are told
of Mushari's reactions to everything he discovers, so it is as if we are
looking at Eliot over Mushari's shoulder. This technique invites readers
to compare Mushari's reactions to their own and challenges them to
come to their own judgments about the novel's characters and events.
By creating a narrative frame for the novel, Vonnegut avoids one of the
most dangerous pitfalls for the satirist. If it is not handled carefully, a
satire can begin to sound like a sermon, as the author points out the sins
of his society and pleads for reform. A preachy tone ruins the laughter
that is satire's most effective weapon (for a detailed discussion of satire,
see chapter 2 of this volume). Placing Mushari between readers and the
story preserves the comic tone and leaves most of the moralizing to the
readers.

As we follow Mushari's investigation, readers discover that Eliot was
born in 1918, the son of Senator Lister Ames Rosewater of Indiana. He
left Harvard Law School in 1941 to volunteer for the infantry in World

War II. After distinguished service in many battles, he was promoted to captain, but late in the war, he suffered a nervous breakdown. While recuperating in Paris, he met and married Sylvia, the beautiful daughter of a wealthy and socially prominent French family. After the war, he returned to the United States, finished his law degree, and was appointed the first president of the Rosewater Foundation. Although supposedly a charitable institution, the foundation is actually an elaborate scheme to pass the Rosewater fortune to subsequent generations without paying taxes on it. As president, Eliot can do as he pleases with the interest on the family fortune, $3,500,000 a year in 1964, but he has no control over the principal.

Between 1947 and 1953, Eliot runs the foundation in a conventional way. He spends a total of fourteen million dollars on a wide variety of worthy causes, including cancer research, studies of mental illness, alcoholism, and racial prejudice, and he buys famous works of art for museums. During these years, Eliot is drinking heavily, but without obvious ill effects, until one day he becomes so drunk that his wife has to come and take him home from the office. A few days later, he leaves on the first of several aimless journeys across the country. He shows up at a science fiction writers' conference and makes a drunken speech in which he claims that science fiction writers are the true poets of our times because they are the only ones who have the courage to tackle the major issues. Before leaving, he gives each of the writers a check for $200 and suggests that they write about the fantastic powers of money in our strange society. Establishing a pattern that he will repeat on his subsequent rambles, Eliot hitchhikes from one small town to the next, offering to buy drinks for anyone who has a volunteer fireman's badge. He trades his expensive suits for the work clothes and cheap suits of the men he drinks with.

Eventually, Eliot ends up in Rosewater County, Indiana, the ancestral home of the Rosewater family, which has never been home to Eliot, who was raised in East Coast prep schools. He calls Sylvia and announces that he has decided to live in the Rosewater mansion and care for the "discarded Americans" of the county, even though they are "useless and unattractive" (44). Sylvia joins him in Rosewater, and they spend the next five years snubbing the middle-class professionals who run the foundation's industries and entertaining "morons, perverts, starvelings and the unemployed" (50). Eliot moves the foundation's headquarters to a filthy office over a diner and begins dispensing comfort, advice, over-the-counter medications, small amounts of money, and unconditional love. After five years of selfless devotion to "the pitiful people of Rose-

water County," Sylvia suffers a nervous breakdown and is institution-
alized, while Eliot carries on the work. Shock treatments and
chemotherapy manage to "cure" Sylvia, and she returns to Europe to
join the international "Jet Set" and forget about Eliot and the people of
Rosewater. She then suffers a relapse, and in 1964, as the present action
of the novel begins, she is suing Eliot for divorce on the advice of her
psychiatrist.

The rest of the novel takes place during three days in June 1964 and
a single day in June 1965. Eliot and Sylvia agree to meet in Indianapolis
to say goodbye and finalize the details of their divorce. The people of
Rosewater mourn the loss of their benefactor, as Eliot becomes increasingly withdrawn from reality, unable to remember the people he has
helped over the years. On the bus to Indianapolis, he sees the city incin-
erated in a firestorm, much like the one that consumed Dresden during
World War II. This hallucination signals Eliot's descent into madness.
The final chapter describes his "awakening" a year later in an insane
asylum in Indianapolis. He learns that while he was out of touch with
reality Norman Mushari filed suit on behalf of Fred Rosewater, and Eliot's sanity hearing is scheduled for the next day. Meanwhile, fifty-seven
women in Rosewater County have claimed that Eliot is the father of their
children. Although none of these allegations are true, Eliot uses them to
put an end to Fred's claim on the foundation. He tells his attorney to
draw up papers recognizing all of the children as his rightful heirs: "Let
their names be Rosewater from this moment on. And tell them that their
father loves them, no matter what they may turn out to be" (275).

CHARACTER DEVELOPMENT

Kurt Vonnegut has been criticized for not creating rounded, believable
characters. Although this criticism is based on an accurate observation,
it seems irrelevant to *God Bless You, Mr. Rosewater* because it is a satire,
and in satire, characters represent recognizable types or stand for various
ideas or social forces (for a discussion of satire, see chapter 2 of this
volume). Vonnegut should not be criticized for failing to accomplish
something that he has not attempted. Instead we should try to understand how Vonnegut's techniques of characterization contribute to this
satire on contemporary American society.

Eliot Rosewater is the novel's protagonist, or main character. Although
he is the heir to a great fortune and a decorated war hero, he is plagued
by the guilt of killing a fourteen-year-old boy during the war. His sanity

is in question from the moment he is introduced to the reader. Vonnegut presents Eliot through the eyes of Norman Mushari, a lawyer who is trying to prove that he is insane, and we are told that in the law office he is commonly referred to as "The Nut" and "The Saint" (5). Eliot's alcoholism, erratic behavior, and total lack of concern about his physical appearance all tend to make the reader doubt his sanity. However, Vonnegut provides multiple perspectives on Eliot that make it more difficult to dismiss him as crazy. His French father-in-law considers him "the sanest American he had ever met" because he recognized the horror and the absurdity of the Second World War (85). Eliot's wife Sylvia points out that the eccentric form of charity he practices in Rosewater County is motivated by his conviction that someone must try to love and care for all the misfits and outcasts of American society. Kilgore Trout, Eliot's favorite science fiction writer, helps Senator Rosewater defend Eliot against charges of insanity by providing rational explanations for most of Eliot's seemingly crazy behavior.

All of these perspectives contribute to our understanding of Eliot's character, but ultimately, readers are forced to evaluate Eliot's ideas and actions for themselves. The "first piece of solid evidence" that Mushari expects will help him prove that Eliot is insane is Eliot's letter to whoever inherits the Rosewater fortune after his death (13). The letter describes how Noah Rosewater accumulated a vast fortune by cheating his brother out of the family business and overcharging the U.S. government for supplies during the Civil War. It goes on to suggest that other large American fortunes were also based on bribery, theft of government property, and the exploitation of workers. From Mushari's point of view, the letter proves that Eliot is crazy because it contradicts the widely accepted myth that great fortunes are the product of individual ingenuity and hard work. But to a reader with any knowledge of American history, Eliot's indictment of the unfairness of American capitalism and the cruelty of the American class system rings true. Maybe Eliot is not the crazy one. Attentive readers come to question the sanity of a system that rewards corruption and punishes honesty and hard work.

Senator Lister Ames Rosewater, Eliot's father, is a conservative politician and moral crusader. He represents the extreme right wing of American politics, so he becomes an important target for Vonnegut's satire. Early in the novel, we are given excerpts from his most famous speech, in which he compares America in the 1950s with Rome in the time of Caesar Augustus. Senator Rosewater claims that in both periods "liberals" led their countries into moral, political, and economic decay and that desperate measures are needed to save civilization. He praises

Caesar for writing "morals into law" and enforcing the laws with harsh penalties, and he regrets that he cannot do the same. Instead he proposes a return to the "Free Enterprise System" that will force everyone to "sink or swim" without any help from the government (31). This is pretty typical conservative rhetoric, and it is even more popular today than it was when Vonnegut wrote this book. The hypocrisy behind the rhetoric is obvious to attentive readers. The senator inherited his fortune, so he never had to "sink or swim." If we recall Eliot's account of how the Rosewater fortune was founded on massive government giveaways facilitated by bribes, the hypocrisy is even more despicable.

Norman Mushari, the lawyer who hopes to transfer control of the Rosewater Foundation, is described as being both physically and morally repulsive. Vonnegut calls him a "boy shyster" who has "an enormous ass, which was luminous when bare" (3). Predictably, he becomes the butt of office jokes. His colleagues nickname him the weasel, and they refuse to socialize with him. But whenever readers might feel tempted to sympathize with this social outcast, Vonnegut reminds us of Mushari's total lack of concern for other people and his willingness to do anything to achieve his selfish goals. He is essentially a minor character whose function in the novel is to keep the plot moving by attempting to transfer control of the Rosewater Foundation. He also provides a particularly repulsive example of the selfish attitudes that the capitalist system encourages.

Fred Rosewater is Eliot's distant cousin and next in line to inherit control of the foundation. He is an overweight insurance salesman in a small Rhode Island town who ekes out a living by convincing working-class men that a life insurance policy is their only hope of providing security for their families. Everything about Fred is pathetic, from his slovenly physical appearance to his poorly disguised lust for the "show-girls" who appear in the tabloid newspaper (136). Fred's wife constantly reminds him of his failure to earn enough money for her to socialize with the wealthy people in town. She keeps him on the verge of bankruptcy with her pursuit of a lifestyle that they cannot afford. Fred represents the desperation of the American middle class. He is trapped in a job that gives him neither dignity nor satisfaction.

Vonnegut contrasts Fred's meaningless, pathetic existence with the virile, active life of Harry Pena. Although Pena was once an insurance salesman like Fred, an accident forced him to work out of doors, so he makes his living as a commercial fisherman. Harry is described as having "a head and shoulders that Michelangelo might have given to Moses or God" (151). Just as the description of Mushari alerts readers that he is a despicable character, so the description of Pena makes it clear that he is to be admired. We are also told that Harry is the chief of the Pisquontuit Volunteer Fire Department and one of the few men in town "whose manhood was not in question" (152). When Fred tries to interest him in a picture of a bikini-clad woman in the tabloid newspaper, Harry reminds him that it is only a picture and points out that if she were real, all he would have to do to make a living is stay at home and cut out pictures of fish. While Fred spends his life shuffling paper, Harry goes out on the ocean as a hunter, as men once did in a more heroic age.

All of the details that come together to define Harry's character make it clear that he represents an earlier and more noble way of being a man. For one thing, his father was a fisherman and he takes his two sons out with him, thus preserving a family tradition and strengthening family ties in a way that most modern jobs do not allow. Fishing provides the men with a direct connection to nature. As they haul their nets, it is a "magic time" and the three men are "purified of all thought" (182). For a moment at least, they have escaped the corruption and meanness so prevalent in the rest of the novel. When their work is done and the fish are on board, they are "as satisfied with life as men can ever be" (184). When Harry Pena's character is presented out of context, it gives a false impression of Vonnegut as a sentimental writer who longs for an earlier time when "men were men" and work meant honest, physical labor out of doors. However, this idyllic fishing scene is witnessed by the idle rich from a seaside restaurant whose owner informs a customer that Harry is bankrupt and that men who work with their hands are hopelessly out of date in the modern world, where "stupid, silly" people seem to be inheriting everything (186).

Stewart and Amanita Buntline fit this description perfectly. Although they are minor characters and their stories are never really woven into the main plot line, they are important to the novel's structure because readers are encouraged to compare them with Eliot and Sylvia Rosewater. Stewart, like Eliot, inherited a large fortune, and, like Eliot, he suffers from guilt for having so much money in a world where so many people are poor. After his first year at Harvard, Stewart approaches the lawyer who manages his trust fund and demands that the money be given away to relieve the suffering of the poor. However, unlike Eliot, Stewart is easily dissuaded from following through on his generous impulse. Convinced that his money would not solve society's problems, he retreats to his mansion by the sea and passes his days reading about the Civil War, taking long naps, and drinking Scotch. He is so inactive that his daughter checks to see if he is alive at least once a day. Occasionally

his lawyer sends him a conservative pamphlet intended to prevent any
further attacks of conscience, but Stewart is too content in his life of
idleness to bother to read them. As Stewart snoozes on his couch, readers
are told that the most recent pamphlet attacks social security and welfare
by claiming that these government programs make people too lazy and
stupid to work. The irony is that this is a better description of Stewart,
and of the effects of inherited wealth, than it is of the welfare system
and its recipients.

Amanita Buntline is Stewart's snobbish, vapid wife. She is carrying on
an affair with Fred's wife Caroline, but she takes every opportunity to
point out her friend's relative poverty and lack of social importance.
Although she claims to love classical music, especially Beethoven, she
cannot tell the difference when her records play at 78 r.p.m. rather than
33. Just as Stewart provides a contrast to Eliot, Amanita's false pretenses
to culture contrast with the sophistication of Eliot's wife, Sylvia.

Sylvia was born in Paris, the daughter of a wealthy patroness of the
arts and an accomplished classical musician. As a girl, she met the lead-
ing artists, writers, and statesmen of the day in her parent's home. She
is described as if she were an extremely sensitive hothouse flower: "A
pale and delicate girl, cultivated, wispy" (43). Sylvia tolerates Eliot's peculiar behavior because she is used to the eccentricities of the European
artists she knew in her youth. She goes with him to Rosewater County
and helps him love the unlovable people there until the strain causes a
nervous breakdown. Her psychiatrist diagnoses her condition as "Samaritrophia," which he defines as "hysterical indifference to the troubles
of those less fortunate than oneself" (51). Months of shock therapy and
medication "cure" her, although her doctor is highly skeptical of the
value of his cure. Sylvia's sensitivity and compassion have been banished, and she becomes a thoughtless, selfish member of the international
"Jet Set," as Europe's wealthy pleasure seekers were known in the 1960s.
Eventually her feelings for Eliot and the people of Rosewater County
return, but her doctor advises that she is not strong enough to go back
to a life of service.

Diana Moon Glampers is the only servant in the Rosewater mansion
in Indiana, and for most of the year, she has the place to herself. Although she is a minor character, she is the best developed of all the
"unlovable" citizens of Rosewater whom Eliot tries so hard to love. The
way she is described makes it clear that Eliot has taken on a difficult
task. She is introduced as a "sixty-eight-year-old virgin who, by almost
anybody's standards, was too dumb to live" (72–73). She has never been
loved by anybody. Plagued by almost constant pain, she is ugly, illiter-

ate, and ignorant of the world outside Rosewater County. Such a pitiful creature might be expected to evoke the reader's sympathy, but Vonnegut seems determined to thwart this reaction by presenting all her afflictions in a comic way. For example, when she describes the kidney pain that torments her, she says "kiddleys" instead of kidneys, and she gives such a hopelessly exaggerated description of the pain that it is impossible to take her seriously. The fact that Eliot *does* take her seriously illustrates his sincere compassion for all of the poor, suffering people in the world. As she launches into an absurd fable about how she was behind the door when the good Lord gave out the brains and the good looks, the reader's laughter contrasts sharply with Eliot's attentive sympathy. Eliot's tender care of Diana Moon Glampers suggests that his nickname "The Saint" may actually be appropriate. So does her testimony about the miraculous cures that Eliot has supposedly performed. Although she is a less-than-reliable source, she claims that Eliot has cured a man who suffered from boils for ten years and that after a visit with Eliot, a woman "threw her crutch away" (78). By putting these words in the mouth of such a limited character, Vonnegut suggests that Eliot is a Christlike figure while undermining the connection at the same time. By making us laugh at a person Eliot takes seriously, Vonnegut invites readers to question Eliot's sanity. But if we reflect more deeply on how our reaction differs from Eliot's, we may decide that Diana Moon Glampers helps us to see the limits of our own compassion.

Kilgore Trout, who appears in seven of Vonnegut's novels, makes his first appearance in *God Bless You, Mr. Rosewater*. He is Eliot's favorite science fiction writer, and one of his novels is summarized early in the book, but we do not see him in person until the final pages of the novel. At Eliot's insistence he has been summoned by Senator Rosewater to help prepare Eliot's defense against the charges of insanity. Trout is an old man who is described as looking like a "kindly country undertaker" (257). Although he is an incredibly prolific writer, he is unable to make a living from his work, so he has taken a job at a stamp redemption center in Hyannis, Massachusetts. Eliot does not recognize him at first because he has shaved off his long beard. Trout explains that it would be sacrilegious for a "Jesus figure" to redeem stamps (267). This humorous remark actually provides one way to look at Trout's role in the novel. He acts as the moral center in a book that is otherwise full of craziness and immorality. He explains the pure motives behind Eliot's bizarre behavior, and he seems to speak for Vonnegut as he drives home the lessons of the novel.

THEMATIC ISSUES

The best way to discuss the themes of *God Bless You, Mr. Rosewater* is to express them in question form and then look for the answers. Of course, the novel rarely provides direct answers, and even these few answers lead to more questions, but that is one of the joys of reading Vonnegut. He suggests several possible answers to every question, then points out their limitations and challenges his readers to think more deeply about the issues he has raised. Another joy of reading Vonnegut is that he deals with serious issues by telling jokes—the more serious the issue, the more complex and funny the joke. Discussing Vonnegut's themes puts one in the unenviable position of explaining his jokes, and everyone knows how disastrous it is to explain a joke. Nevertheless, it is the only way to approach the central questions raised in *God Bless You, Mr. Rosewater*: How do we define sanity and insanity? What responsibility do we have toward other human beings? How can people build meaningful lives in a world where machines do most of the work?

Since the plot of the novel involves an attempt to prove that Eliot Rosewater is insane, we are faced with the question What do we mean when we say that someone is insane? The simple answer is that an insane person behaves in an abnormal way, but this answer forces us to define what we mean by "normal," and the definition of normal behavior depends on the society in which a person lives. The story of Eliot Rosewater forces readers to question his sanity, but ultimately it forces them to reconsider the sanity of contemporary American society.

Eliot's abnormal behavior begins shortly after he kills a fourteen-year-old boy during World War II. He lies down in front of a truck and is nearly killed. When his comrades reach his side, he is totally rigid and unable to move. He refuses to eat or sleep and is transferred to a Paris mental hospital. His ailment would have been called "shell shock" in World War I, "battle fatigue" in World War II, and "post-traumatic stress disorder" in Vietnam, but regardless of the name, it is considered a mental disorder brought on by the horrors of war. But the novel does not allow readers to dismiss Eliot as insane. Sylvia tells us that her father considered Eliot "the sanest American he had ever met" because he was the only one who had "noticed" the war (85). By emphasizing Eliot's nationality, Sylvia's father calls attention to the dominant role society plays in defining sanity. By claiming that other Americans have not noticed the war, he suggests that Eliot's mental collapse is a more appropriate response to the horrors of war than the numb indifference that allowed others to fight on. If the world has gone crazy, the only "sane" response may be a retreat into insanity.

Sylvia's battle with mental illness also leads us to question the sanity of modern American society. The psychiatrist who attempts to cure her must first decide what constitutes "normal" behavior. Because he believes her nervous breakdown was brought on by an overactive conscience, he must determine how much "normal" people care about others. His conclusion is that a "normal person, functioning well on the upper levels of a prosperous, industrialized society, can hardly hear his conscience at all" (54). This is an example of indirect satire at its best. At first, Sylvia seems to be the target of the satire. She represents the wealthy woman so far removed from the cares of the real world that she is not strong enough to function in it. Then it appears that her psychiatrist is the target. His diagnosis of "Samaritrophia" makes fun of the excessive jargon in his profession, and he seems more than a little crazy himself. But Vonnegut has bigger game in his sights. What kind of a society do we have if, to be considered normal, a person must stifle her conscience? The clear implication of this tale of mental illness is that our society is sick and in need of treatment. *God Bless You, Mr. Rosewater* is satiric shock treatment for our crazy modern world.

Sylvia's story also relates to the second thematic question that *God Bless You, Mr. Rosewater* raises: What responsibility do we have toward other human beings? Some characters have no trouble answering this question. Senator Rosewater believes that the rich deserve everything they have and sharing anything with the poor will only make them lazy. Stewart Buntline's lawyer persuades him to adopt the same attitude. More thoughtful characters, like Eliot and Sylvia, wrestle with the enormous responsibility that great wealth brings. Although the Rosewater Foundation was originally designed to cheat the government out of inheritance taxes, Eliot takes its philanthropic mission seriously. Sylvia provides the best explanation of the motives behind Eliot's philanthropic experiment in her meeting with Senator Rosewater and the foundation's lawyers. She refuses to dismiss Eliot as insane and insists that what he is doing is noble, in spite of the fact that she cannot think of anything good to say about the people Eliot is trying to help. When the senator continues to demand an explanation, she finally admits, "The secret is they're human" (68). At this point, the satire comes dangerously close to a sermon on the universal brotherhood of mankind, but once again Vonnegut preserves the satiric tone by ending the scene with a joke. As Sylvia looks into the faces of her listeners, hoping to see a sign that they have understood the importance of her statement, she is disappointed. When at last she looks at Norman Mushari, he gives her a "hideously inappropriate smile of greed and fornication" (69). The inappropriate reactions of the men place one of the novel's central themes in an ironic frame. If these powerful men cannot understand the importance of our common humanity, there is little reason to hope that our corrupt society will be reformed any time soon. The novel shows how difficult it is for us to love our fellow humans, and it also shows how important it is to try.

Vonnegut often seems to be offering Eliot as an example of selfless behavior, but Eliot does so many crazy things that it is hard to take him seriously as a role model. He realizes that the poor people of Rosewater need more than money. They need to feel loved. They need to feel that they are productive and important members of society. Eliot recognizes these needs, and he responds as best he can, listening to Diana Moon Glampers's endless tales of woe and trying to come up with activities that will occupy the empty hours of the people who seek his help. But the chaos that follows his departure from Rosewater County reveals that he has failed to make a lasting, positive difference in the lives of its residents. Even his final gesture, which makes fifty-seven babies heirs to his fortune, is unlikely to make any real difference in their lives. The novel suggests that they will become like Stewart and Amanita Buntline, whose lives are empty and meaningless in spite of their wealth.

Eliot's experiment is an exercise in paternalism because he tries to be a loving father to everyone he meets. Not only is this exhausting for Eliot, in the long run it does little for the people of Rosewater. In this case the senator is right: giving people things just makes them dependent. Money, or the lack of it, is not the real problem, nor can it be the solution. The novel's most important issue is raised in the final pages by Kilgore Trout, who asks, "How to love people who have no use?" (264). Trout sees Eliot's failed experiment as an attempt to find an answer to this question, which is a major concern of Vonnegut's fiction from *Player Piano*, his first novel, right through to *Timequake*, his last. Of course, *God Bless You, Mr. Rosewater* does not provide a clear answer, but it does give us some important clues.

Early in the novel, Eliot's obsession with volunteer fire departments seems to be little more than another symptom of his mental decline. But as he continues to visit fire stations all over the country, his fascination is explained in a number of ways, and each explanation provides a clue as to how human life could be improved. As a boy, Eliot was the "mascot" of the Rosewater County Volunteer Fire Department, and he has fond memories of ringing the fire bell and riding on the trucks. Too many children lack this kind of loving attention, and it is essential if they are to grow into confident, caring adults. The firemen also remind Eliot of the men he knew in the war, and he sees them as patriotic Americans willing to defend the nation's values (25). Their dedication to their country gives them a greater purpose and helps them overcome the sense of hopelessness that plagues individuals who care only about their own prosperity. On the other hand, the volunteer firemen also bring up horrible wartime memories of the German fire fighters that Eliot killed. In the midst of a war, they were battling to saves lives and property, so they became symbols of goodness struggling against evil. Killing them taught Eliot that war itself is the enemy and that all men must be treated as brothers.

In the final pages of the novel, Kilgore Trout adds another explanation for Eliot's love of volunteer fire departments. He points out that they are a rare example of "enthusiastic unselfishness" because the fire fighters are willing to risk their lives to save others, and "from this we must learn" (266). *God Bless You, Mr. Rosewater* offers attentive readers many opportunities to learn valuable lessons about life in modern American society. The novel shows just how crazy our nation has become and offers a few clues about how we can return to sanity, without ever underestimating the difficulty of meaningful reform. It demonstrates the importance of compassion by showing how empty life is without meaningful connections to other people. But any statement of the novel's themes is bound to seem inadequate to readers who fully appreciate the novel's spirit. *God Bless You, Mr. Rosewater* prompts us to question the world around us, to ask why there is so much suffering, and to keep asking questions until we find satisfying answers.

A MARXIST READING

Since the fall of the Soviet Union, many people assume that Marxism is dead and has nothing to say about the world we live in. Nothing could be farther from the truth. At its core, Marxism contains a critique of capitalism that is just as valid today as it was in the nineteenth century, when it was formulated by German philosopher/economist Karl Marx in two books, *The German Ideology* (1845) and *The Communist Manifesto* (1848). Marxism began as a theory of historical and economic change, not as a literary theory, and Marx had little to say about the relationship between his ideas and literature. However, because Marxism provides a

comprehensive theory of human history and describes how social institutions influence our view of the world, it has been applied to the study
of literature.

Marx said that the source of human misery is the struggle between the
rich and the poor. As long as there are separate classes of people with
conflicting interests, the world will be a battleground, and people will
be unable to realize their full potential. Marx claimed that the economic
system of a society creates and controls all other human institutions,
including the legal system, schools, politics, religion, even art and literature. In a capitalist society, all of these institutions serve the rich and
help them to maintain their power over the poor by convincing people
that there is no viable alternative to the way things are. Marx referred
to the system of beliefs and values that the rich use to control the poor
as their "ideology." Because literature is a part of this ideology, it may
be analyzed from a Marxist point of view in much the same way that
religion, politics, and the law are analyzed. Marxist critics attempt to
determine the author's personal ideology and then compare it with the
prevailing ideology of the time to determine whether the author supports
or opposes the capitalist system.

Marx pointed out that capitalism encourages the division of labor. In
a pre-capitalist economy, a shoemaker measured his customer's foot, cut
and stitched the leather, and nailed on the sole. He did everything that
needed to be done to make a shoe, and he also knew his customers. As
shoe factories began to replace individual shoemakers, workers became
more and more specialized. No longer were they responsible for the
entire process of making a shoe, nor did they know the people who were
buying the shoes they made. More importantly, they lost control over
the process, and with this loss of control came a diminished sense of
satisfaction with work and a growing feeling of alienation from other
workers. Marx claims that alienation, a feeling that one is cut off from
meaningful contact with others, is one of the worst things about the
capitalist system because it robs workers of a sense of purpose and reduces them to the status of machines serving the interests of the rich.

A Marxist reading of God Bless You, Mr. Rosewater will highlight certain
aspects of the text while ignoring others. The obvious place to start is
with the novel's depiction of how the ideology of the rich is forced on
the working class. This will help us to determine Vonnegut's ideology
so that we can see how it compares to Marxism. Senator Rosewater's
"Golden Age of Rome" speech provides a perfect example of capitalist
ideology. The senator claims that people are poor because they will not
work. But, as Eliot has already pointed out, workers are kept in poverty

because the rich refuse to pay them adequate wages. By placing the senator's speech after Eliot's more convincing explanation of poverty, the novel reveals how capitalist ideology blames the victims of the system as a way of shifting responsibility away from the rich.

Selena Deal, the Buntlines' upstairs maid, is a minor character in the novel, but Vonnegut uses her to strike a major blow against capitalist ideology. Before becoming the Buntlines' maid, she lived in the orphanage set up by Stewart Buntline's great-grandfather. Every week the orphans are required to take an oath that they will "respect the sacred private property of others" (189). In capitalist ideology, private property is considered sacred in order to justify the fact that some people are rich and others are poor. The connection between capitalism and Christianity is made more obvious as the oath goes on. The orphans are told to be content with their role in life because it has been assigned to them by God. They must respect the rich because God has placed them on a higher level. If they serve the rich faithfully and well, they will be rewarded in heaven. If not, they will roast in hell. As Marx pointed out, capitalism allies itself with Christianity in order to convince workers that an unjust system is actually God's will. Although this is one of the most common and effective strategies of capitalist ideology, Vonnegut ridicules it simply by stating it in very basic terms.

In a letter to the head of the orphanage, Selena exposes the emptiness of the Buntlines' lives. They have no appreciation for art or music and instead become obsessed with their daughter's sailboat races. Vonnegut's depiction of the Buntlines is in keeping with Marx's idea that even the lives of the rich are affected by the alienation that capitalism causes. But what really bothers Selena about the Buntlines is not their pointless lives but the attitude they have toward anyone who is not rich. They think that "everything nice in the world is a gift to the poor people from them or their ancestors" (194). In an effort to please Mrs. Buntline, Selena actually thanks her for a particularly beautiful sunset. Capitalist ideology typically describes the wealthy as generous benefactors of the poor. Marx pointed out that all wealth comes from the labor of the working class and what the rich give back is nothing compared to what they have taken. Vonnegut makes the same point in a much more amusing way by having Mrs. Buntline expect that Selena will thank her for the sunset.

Marxists believe that society can be changed for the better if we take a close look at its economic foundations. Eliot Rosewater proposes just such a careful examination to a group of science fiction writers when he interrupts one of their conferences. He asks them to put aside tales of distant galaxies and creatures with strange powers to consider the equally odd powers that the rich have on this planet. He points out that even though he was "born naked, just like you," he now has thousands of dollars a day to spend (23). He illustrates his point by writing each of them a check for $200 and asking them to think about better ways to circulate money. Eliot's speech reveals the fundamental unfairness of a system in which some babies are born rich and others are born poor. *God Bless You, Mr. Rosewater* can be read as Vonnegut's attempt to write a book like the one Eliot describes. The novel consistently criticizes the capitalist system and offers ideas about how the system could be improved.

So far, Vonnegut's ideology seems to be entirely consistent with Marxist theory, but Vonnegut is no Marxist. Although both Marx and Vonnegut criticize the capitalist system, they have different ideas about what should replace it. Marx said that eventually the workers will revolt against the rich and seize power. Then they will turn control of the economic system over to the government which will run it for the worker's benefit, creating a system that Marx called socialism. Marx saw socialism as a transitional period that would lead to a "worker's paradise" that he called communism. Under communism, the government would no longer be necessary because people would govern themselves, working together and sharing equally in the fruits of their labor.

Vonnegut is not so optimistic about the future. Although he obviously believes that people must learn to share the wealth, he does not see a revolution happening any time soon. The book as a whole suggests that even if the workers revolted, they would be unlikely to replace capitalism with anything better. Although Kilgore Trout, who often seems to speak for Vonnegut, calls himself a socialist, a Marxist critic would fault Vonnegut for not clearly advocating socialism as the cure for what ails America. But is this really a fault with Vonnegut's novel, or does it reveal more about the narrowness of Marxist theory? Vonnegut's vision of the world is too complex and ironic to stay within the boundaries established by Karl Marx. Even though he might like to believe that a worker's paradise is possible, Vonnegut sees human nature too clearly to have much faith that it will ever arrive. For a Marxist critic, this lack of faith is a fatal flaw in Vonnegut's ideology, but it is also what makes him one of the most thought-provoking novelists of our time.

Slaughterhouse-Five
(1969)

Slaughterhouse-Five is Kurt Vonnegut's best-known novel, and it made his reputation as a major American writer. Based on Vonnegut's experiences as a prisoner of war in Germany during the Second World War, *Slaughterhouse-Five* was published at the height of American military involvement in Vietnam. The novel's strong anti-war message appealed to readers who were disillusioned with America's crusade against communism. Mixing brutal realism with science fiction, *Slaughterhouse-Five* challenges readers to make sense of a world gone mad. Billy Pilgrim, the novel's protagonist, is a hapless American private who is neither physically nor mentally fit to be a soldier. From his perspective, war is not a heroic contest between the forces of good and evil but a senseless slaughter with many victims and no villains. As Billy tries to cope with life after the war, readers come to appreciate the full cost of armed conflict. But *Slaughterhouse-Five* is not just a moving account of one man's experience during World War II. It is also a book about America in the 1960s. Vonnegut portrays a nation that has betrayed its founding principles of democracy, freedom, justice, and opportunity for all. By calling for a return to these principles, Vonnegut engaged the conscience of a generation and wrote a novel that is widely regarded as an American classic.

NARRATIVE TECHNIQUE

In *Slaughterhouse-Five*, Kurt Vonnegut invented a new way of telling a story. After years of struggling to describe his experiences as a prisoner of war in conventional ways, he realized that the attempt was futile. A typical plot structure is based on a conflict between characters that builds to a climax and is then resolved. Vonnegut realized that although his story was full of conflict, it really had no climax, and in the end, nothing was resolved. Furthermore, conventional storytelling techniques encourage writers to glorify war by concentrating on the heroic exploits of their characters. Experience taught Vonnegut that real wars rob people of the ability to act heroically. He could not make the people he knew during the war into conventional literary characters and still be true to his own experience.

The first chapter of *Slaughterhouse-Five* describes Vonnegut's struggle with narrative technique. He makes outlines that trace the lives of his characters in chronological order. He considers where the climax of his story should come, finally settling on the execution of Edgar Derby for stealing a teapot in the ruins of Dresden. But somehow these conventional narrative techniques do not do justice to the story he wants to tell. A visit to his old army buddy and fellow prisoner of war Bernard V. O'Hare helps him see where he is going wrong. O'Hare's wife Mary is clearly upset by Vonnegut's visit. Convinced that his novel will glorify war and make young people eager to fight, she reminds Vonnegut that most soldiers are really children, much younger than the middle-aged men who star in war movies, and that he has a responsibility as a parent to discourage future wars. Moved by Mary's words, Vonnegut vows to tell his story in such a way that readers will see war for the senseless slaughter that it is. He decides to call the book *The Children's Crusade*, which eventually became the novel's subtitle, and this makes him curious about the crusades of the Middle Ages. O'Hare pulls out a copy of Charles MacKay's 1841 book *Extraordinary Popular Delusions and the Madness of Crowds*, which includes a chapter on the crusades. MacKay compares the way that the crusaders are described in history books with the portrait of them that emerges from romances, an early form of prose fiction that was popular in the fifteenth and sixteenth centuries. Historians tell us that the crusaders were ignorant, cruel men who fought for their own material advantage rather than for the glory of God. On the other hand, romances describe the crusaders as pure, pious heroes who fought with great honor and courage. Vonnegut certainly does not want to glorify war, as the romances do, but neither does he want to demonize those who fought in the modern crusade to rid the world of Nazism. As a student of anthropology after the war, he was taught that "nobody was ridiculous or bad or disgusting" (10). Vonnegut took this lesson to heart, and it makes him reluctant to create the villains that conventional storytelling requires. Instead, he helps readers understand why people behave monstrously, without resorting to the simple solution of calling them monsters.

Having discarded traditional ways of telling a story, Vonnegut has to invent a new way that will allow him to overcome another obstacle: the fallibility of human memory. When he and O'Hare sit down to reminisce about the war, they discover that they recall only insignificant details. If he cannot clearly recall an event as important as the fire bombing of Dresden, how can Vonnegut hope to give readers an accurate impression of his wartime experiences? His surprising solution to this problem is to give his protagonist, Billy Pilgrim, the ability to travel in time. Time travel allows Vonnegut to create the impression that readers are looking at events as they happen, rather than through the mists of memory. But because most readers do not believe in time travel, the technique also highlights the artificiality of any writing about the past. While a conventional novel gives readers the illusion of a clear and accurate depiction of events, *Slaughterhouse-Five* constantly reminds us that we are reading fiction. Yet Vonnegut begins the book by claiming, "All this happened, more or less," and he often comments on his own presence at crucial moments in the story (1). *Slaughterhouse-Five* is a curious hybrid of fact and fiction that insists on its factual truth even as it uses fantastic fictional techniques.

Mixing fact and fantasy and jumping around in time allow Vonnegut to overcome another obstacle to telling his story: "There is nothing intelligent to say about a massacre" (24). Vonnegut has stated repeatedly that he does not want to argue with those who claim the bombing of Dresden was justified by the Holocaust and other Nazi atrocities. Perhaps it would be more accurate to say that he does not want to debate this point directly. Jumping around in time allows Vonnegut to juxtapose short, vivid scenes and leave it up to the reader to make the connections between them. Yet the scenes are so artfully arranged that readers must question whether revenge for even the most terrible atrocities could justify the slaughter of so many human beings.

Vonnegut realizes that his new method of storytelling places great demands on the reader, and he does his best to lighten the burden by providing a brief biography of Billy Pilgrim early in the book. Born in Ilium, New York, in 1922, the same year as Vonnegut, Billy is the only child of a barber. In his youth he is weak and "funny looking" (30). After graduating in the top third of his high-school class, he is drafted, serves in the army, and is taken prisoner by the Germans. Back in Ilium after the war, he goes to optometry school and becomes engaged to the daughter of the school's founder and owner. After suffering a nervous breakdown, he marries his fiancée and becomes a successful optometrist. He has two children. His daughter Barbara marries an optometrist, and his son Robert overcomes a troubled youth by joining the Green Berets and fighting in Vietnam. On his way to an optometrists' convention, Billy's plane crashes and he is the only survivor. While he is in the hospital, his wife dies of carbon monoxide poisoning. Billy returns to a quiet life in Ilium, but then he goes to New York City, gets on a radio talk show, and tells the world that he was kidnapped by aliens from Tralfamadore, who put him in a zoo with Montana Wildhack, a former movie actress. After returning to Ilium, Billy writes letters to the local paper describing the Tralfamadorians and their concept of time. Armed with this chronological sketch of Billy's life, readers are better prepared to make sense of the novel's abrupt time shifts. Vonnegut also makes the narrative easier to follow by presenting Billy's wartime experiences in chronological order, with one small exception at the end. This keeps the emphasis on the war and prevents the other moments from becoming too distracting.

PLOT DEVELOPMENT

Billy says he first became "unstuck in time" during the Battle of the Bulge, the last big German offensive of World War II, in December 1944. Billy never had a strong will to live, and caught behind enemy lines without a helmet or combat boots, he wants to give up and die. He constantly falls behind his three companions, two unnamed scouts and Roland Weary, an anti-tank gunner. Leaning against a tree with his eyes closed, he sees the "full arc of his life," from birth to death and beyond, before entering a terrifying moment from his childhood (54). His father has brought him to the YMCA to teach him to swim by the "sink-or-swim" method (55). He pitches Billy into the pool, and Billy sinks to the bottom and passes out. He resents his rescuers for saving his life. This scene has obvious parallels with Billy's situation in the war: the terror, the nearness of death, and Billy's resentment toward those who would save him against his will. This first example of time travel establishes the pattern for the rest of the book. Stressful moments cause Billy to travel in time to events with some relationship to the situation he finds himself in during the war.

After the two scouts leave them behind, Billy and Roland Weary are captured by the Germans and marched to a prisoner collection point. A German news photographer takes a picture of Billy's ruined civilian shoes to demonstrate how poorly equipped the American army is, "despite its reputation for being rich" (74). Then the photographer stages a photograph of Billy's capture, and Billy finds himself traveling in time to a hot summer day in 1967. On his way to lunch at the Lions Club in his air-conditioned Cadillac, Billy stops at a red light in the middle of Ilium's black ghetto, a month after much of it has burned in a riot. A black man taps on Billy's window, but when the light changes, Billy simply drives on. Although there is no obvious connection between Billy's experience with the German photographer and the incident in 1967, both involve a contrast between an image of America as a rich country and the often-overlooked reality of widespread poverty. The wartime photos are intended as propaganda, and they obviously distort the truth, but at the same time, they reveal a deeper truth that is mirrored by Billy's brief glimpse of the ghetto.

The speaker at the Lions Club meeting is a marine major who has done two tours of duty in Vietnam. He advocates bombing the North Vietnamese relentlessly until they admit that stronger nations should not be allowed to "force their way of life on weak countries" (76). Of course, that is exactly what the United States is trying to do to the Vietnamese. The major is blind to the preposterous irony of his statement, and so is Billy, who does not protest the bombing, in spite of what he saw in Dresden. Vonnegut's passive protagonist leaves protest up to the reader.

After a few more scenes from 1967 describing Billy's wealthy but spiritually empty life, he returns to the war as the Germans are sorting American prisoners before placing them in railroad cars for the trip to the prison camp. A delirious colonel with double pneumonia, who "lost" an entire regiment of 4,500 men, gives an impassioned speech to his "boys," telling them to be proud of their exploits on the battlefield (84–85). Calling himself "Wild Bob," as he had always hoped his men would, he promises to barbecue whole steers at a regimental reunion after the war. Vonnegut punctuates this tragically false war story by saying "I was there" (86). Wild Bob is such a vivid character, and he illustrates Vonnegut's central themes so clearly, that readers are likely to dismiss him as an invention. By insisting that he heard Wild Bob give this speech, Vonnegut breaks with conventional techniques of fiction to reinforce his readers' sense of the essential truthfulness of his war story, as opposed to the glorification of war so typical in fiction.

After two days of waiting in a packed railroad car, Billy Pilgrim's train slowly begins to move. His ten-day trip to the prison camp is interrupted by a lengthy account of his abduction by Tralfamadorians in 1967, on the eve of his daughter's wedding. While he waits for the aliens to arrive, Billy watches a World War II movie about a bombing raid over Germany. By traveling slowly backwards in time, he watches the movie from the end to the beginning. From Billy's unique perspective, the destruction of the city is miraculously reversed by bombers who then fly backwards to their base. By reversing the typical war story, Vonnegut emphasizes that destruction cannot be so easily repaired in real life. When the Tralfamadorians arrive, Billy asks why he has been chosen, and they reply that his question is meaningless and typical of earthlings. From their perspective, things happen without reason, free will is an illusion, and all creatures are like bugs trapped in the amber of each inevitable moment. This idea is often referred to as "fatalism," since everything that happens is thought to have been fated to happen in advance. Although Tralfamadorian fatalism may seem to describe Billy's helpless situation in the boxcar on the way to the prison camp, the novel consistently demonstrates that human beings have important choices to make. Even in the boxcar, the men can choose to behave generously, as they do when the food comes in, or they can turn on each other and make their situation even worse.

Vonnegut juxtaposes Billy's slow journey to the Nazi prison camp with his incredibly fast trip to Tralfamadore, and attentive readers will notice the parallels between Tralfamadorian fatalism and the Nazis' outlook on life. Shortly after their arrival at the camp, one of the American prisoners makes an offensive comment that is overheard by one of the guards. The guard slugs him, knocking out two teeth. The astonished American asks the same question that Billy Pilgrim posed to the Tralfamadorians, "Why me?" He receives essentially the same answer, "Vy you? Vy anybody?" (116). Like the Tralfamadorians, the Nazis deny the importance of individual choice, which allows them to avoid assuming responsibility for their actions.

After ten days crammed inside a boxcar with little food and water, the miserable Americans arrive at a prison camp where they are greeted by a group of "lusty, ruddy" English officers who have been prisoners since early in the war (118). The contrast between the two groups could not be more striking. The Englishmen are well-fed, healthy, middle-aged, professional soldiers who have spent most of the war lifting weights and playing games. All of the Americans are filthy and starving, and most are really just boys who are still suffering from the shock of their capture. Anticipating a group of prisoners much like themselves, but with the added distinction of being "fresh" from glorious combat, the Englishmen have prepared a feast from their enormous surplus of Red Cross food (121). Having spent most of the war in prison, the Englishmen have imagined that the war was being fought by middle-aged, career soldiers like themselves. They are shocked to see how young and unfit most of the American prisoners are, and one refers to the war as "the Children's Crusade," echoing Vonnegut's subtitle (135).

While staying with the Englishmen, Billy becomes hysterical and is hospitalized. Under the influence of morphine, he travels in time to many different points in his life, including his stay in a Veterans Administration (VA) Hospital in 1948 after he suffered a nervous breakdown. There he meets Eliot Rosewater, the protagonist of Vonnegut's 1965 novel *God Bless You, Mr. Rosewater* (for a discussion of this novel, see chapter 7 of this volume). Rosewater introduces Billy to the science fiction novels of Kilgore Trout. Like Billy, Rosewater finds life "meaningless," and he is trying to "re-invent" himself and his world with the help of science fiction (128). Rosewater tells Billy the story of a Trout novel that features an alien who resembles a Tralfamadorian, evidently planting the seed that will blossom in Billy's fantasy of alien abduction. When his mother visits him in the VA hospital, Billy hides under his blanket because she makes him feel "embarrassed and ungrateful and weak" merely because she is his mother. Billy rejects life, so he has no choice but to reject the woman who gave him life. Billy's fiancée, Valencia Merble, also visits him in the hospital. She is a fat, "ugly," young woman who munches candy bars all day (137). Billy cannot understand why he proposed to her, but he considers the proposal a sure sign that he is going crazy.

From the VA hospital, Billy travels in time to a zoo on Tralfamadore where he has been on display under a geodesic dome for six months. He asks his captors, who seem to live in peace, how wars can be prevented on earth. They reply that preventing wars is impossible. All one can do is "ignore them" and concentrate on the good moments (150). Then Billy travels to his wedding night, six months after his stay in the VA hospital. After they make love and conceive their first child, Valencia asks Billy to tell her about his experiences in the war. The narrator comments that her request reflects a common, "simple-minded" association between "sex and glamor" and war. Billy is reluctant to talk about the war, but as she questions him about the execution of Edgar Derby, he suddenly thinks of an appropriate epitaph for himself, and Vonnegut adds that it would make a good epitaph for him, too. On the next page is a drawing of a gravestone featuring a fat, grinning cherub ascending on stubby wings over these words: "Everything was beautiful and nothing hurt" (156).

When Billy finally returns to the war, the English officers are thoroughly disgusted by the unruly behavior of the American prisoners. A German major tries to explain why the Americans lack discipline and self-respect by reading a report written by Howard W. Campbell, Jr., an American Nazi who is the protagonist of Vonnegut's 1962 novel *Mother Night* (for a discussion of this novel, see chapter 5 of this volume). Campbell states that Americans mistakenly believe it is easy to become rich and that poor people fail because they are stupid. The poor blame themselves for their failure, so they hate themselves and everyone else. According to Campbell, the American army reinforces the self-hatred of the poor by giving its enlisted men shoddy uniforms, while its officers, drawn from the ranks of the rich, are "dashingly-clad" (166). Campbell explains that this is why American prisoners of war behave like "sulky" children (166). Vonnegut uses Campbell, the American Nazi, to deliver his most direct attack on the American class system and the myth of easy wealth that sustains it. Readers are naturally suspicious of the words of an American Nazi, and Campbell's tone reveals contempt for the nation of his birth, but he hits his targets.

Billy falls asleep listening to Campbell's report and wakes up in 1968, where his daughter is accusing him of acting like a child. Billy has embarrassed her by writing crazy letters to the newspaper about his experiences on Tralfamadore, and she is threatening to put him in a rest home. From there he travels to the restful home on Tralfamadore that he shares with Montana Wildhack, whose "baroque" body reminds him of the beautiful city of Dresden before it was bombed (170). Billy's fantasy of living in a zoo on Tralfamadore is his way of returning to innocence. He and Montana are naked all the time. As the only two humans on a strange new planet, they are like Adam and Eve. The comparison between Montana's body and Dresden's architecture reveals Billy's desire to return to a time before the fall of man brought cruelty and destruction to the world.

When Billy returns to the war, Paul Lazarro, a despicable American prisoner who was a car thief before the war, is describing the pleasures of revenge in gruesome detail. For Lazarro, revenge is a personal matter, so he is not especially pleased by the destruction of Dresden. Because Vonnegut mentions this, readers are reminded that one of the motives for bombing Dresden was revenge for German bombing raids on England. Lazarro makes the concept of revenge so unattractive that readers are unlikely to accept it as a justification for the destruction of Dresden. Lazarro threatens to have Billy killed after the war because Roland Weary, the soldier Billy was captured with, blamed Billy for his death and asked Lazarro to seek revenge. Lazarro's threats prompt Billy to travel in time to his death in 1976. By then, Billy has become famous as the prophet of Tralfamadorian fatalism, and he is addressing an enthusiastic crowd in Chicago. As he nears the end of his speech, he declares that the time has come for him to die. Although his followers protest, he reminds them that Tralfamadorians consider every event inevitable. Sure enough, Lazarro kills him with a laser gun.

Billy returns to life in the prison hospital and is told that he has recovered. Billy, Edgar Derby, and Paul Lazarro rejoin the other Americans, who are sleeping in a makeshift theater where the English officers performed a musical version of *Cinderella* the night before. The floor is crammed with sleeping soldiers, so the three newcomers have to sleep on the stage. Without blankets or mattresses, they pull down the azure curtains used in the play and make them into nests. Billy notices another remnant of the play, a pair of boots painted silver to represent Cinderella's magic slippers. Since his shoes are ruined, he tries them on and they fit perfectly. An English officer tells the Americans that they will soon be sent to Dresden, an "open city" with no war industries, so they need not fear an Allied bombing raid (186). To keep warm on the trip to Dresden, Billy wraps himself in the azure curtain of the theater, fashioning a sort of toga. In his toga and silver boots, he is a ridiculous parody of a soldier. He leads a parade of bedraggled American prisoners through the streets of Dresden to the slaughterhouse that will be their home for the next few months.

Then Billy travels in time to the doomed flight to the optometrists' convention in 1968. Although he knows the plane will crash, Billy does not want to appear foolish by refusing to go. On the plane, the optometrists amuse themselves by singing derogatory, sexually explicit songs about Polish people, and the narrator mentions that Billy saw a Polish man hanged during the war for having had sex with a German woman. As the optometrists sing an old minstrel song, the plane crashes into Sugarbush Mountain, a ski resort in Vermont. Billy is rescued by ski instructors wearing black masks who remind him of the white entertainers who put on black makeup to mock African Americans in minstrel shows. From the "Polack" song to the minstrel references, the entire scene highlights the destructive consequences of racist stereotypes (197).

Back in the Dresden slaughterhouse, Howard W. Campbell, Jr., appears in person to ask the American prisoners to join the Nazis and fight against the Russians. Edgar Derby gives an impassioned speech denouncing Campbell, praising American ideals of "freedom and justice," and vowing that Americans and Russians will fight together like brothers to "crush" the Nazis (209). Derby's speech is cut short by air raid sirens that send the Americans underground to a storage room deep beneath the slaughterhouse. In a more conventional narrative, the firebombing of Dresden would follow, but Vonnegut makes his readers wait, explaining that this was actually the night before the raid, and the bombers were bound for other German cities. Down in the shelter, Billy dozes and travels in time to his eighteenth wedding anniversary. He is hosting a party for a group of optometrists and Kilgore Trout, his favorite science fiction writer. A barbershop quartet entertains the group, but something about their performance troubles Billy deeply. He retreats to his bedroom and recalls the night of the Dresden air raid. Billy does not travel in time to the event; he remembers it "shimmeringly" (226). After the city has been destroyed, the American prisoners leave the shelter, and their guards look with horror on the ruins of their city. Rolling their eyes and opening their mouths wide without saying anything, the four guards resemble a barbershop quartet. By presenting this scene as a deeply repressed memory that only returns to Billy after being triggered by the barbershop quartet, Vonnegut calls attention to the way that the human mind buries the most traumatic experiences under the rubble of many insignificant details. The story of the next few days in the ruins of Dresden also emerges indirectly, rather than through time travel, as Billy tells it to Montana Wildhack in the zoo on Tralfamadore. The survivors have no choice but to pick their way across the treacherous rubble, which resembles the surface of the moon. Eventually they arrive at an inn in the suburbs and are given shelter in the stable.

Billy's brief but moving account of the utter destruction he witnessed is followed by the story of how his wife died on the way to visit him in the hospital in Vermont after the plane crash. Grief stricken by his accident, she misses the exit from the highway, slams on her breaks, and is rear-ended by a Mercedes. Her Cadillac loses its exhaust system in the crash, so by the time she arrives at the hospital, she is a "heavenly azure" color from carbon monoxide poisoning (234). The account of her accident is hilarious, and it provides comic relief after the story of Dresden, but it does end with Valencia's death, and significant details link this story with Billy's experiences during the war. Her azure color recalls Billy's ridiculous toga. Like many victims of the Holocaust, she is killed by gas.

The sound that her car makes after the accident is likened to an airplane limping home after being damaged in a bombing raid, and of course the Mercedes that causes the damage is a German car.

Billy shares his hospital room with Bertram Copeland Rumfoord, a Harvard history professor who is also the U.S. Air Force's official historian. He is working on the *Official History of the Army Air Force in World War Two*, and he is having trouble recounting the Dresden air raid, which was hardly mentioned in previous histories. Rumfoord's young wife Lily brings him reference books, and Vonnegut quotes these in order to show the official version of why Dresden was bombed. All of the arguments justifying the raid boil down to this: They started it, and look what they did to us, so they deserved it. When Billy overhears Rumfoord and Lily talking about Dresden, he says, "I was there" (245). Because of Billy's head injury, Rumfoord considers him less than human, and at first, he refuses to believe that he was actually in Dresden. But Billy's persistence convinces him, and eventually he listens to Billy's eyewitness account of the devastation. The official histories treat human casualties as if they were simply numbers in an equation—135,000 dead in Dresden is less significant than 5,000,000 Allied soldiers killed because of German aggression. Vonnegut reminds his readers that every number represents a real human being. His most powerful weapon is the simple act of witness—"I was there."

The final chapter returns to the autobiographical, first-person style of the first chapter. It also brings readers back to the time period in which the book was written by mentioning the recent assassinations of Robert F. Kennedy and Martin Luther King, Jr., and the nightly body count from the war in Vietnam. The novel ends with Billy Pilgrim traveling back in time to one of Vonnegut's most gruesome war experiences, digging into the rubble of Dresden to remove rotting corpses. The execution of Edgar Derby, which Vonnegut once considered his story's climax, is mentioned once more in passing, but now, it is an anti-climax. The end of the war is heralded by a profound silence, punctuated by a bird's poignant, wordless question: "Poo-tee-weet?"

CHARACTER DEVELOPMENT

At one point in *Slaughterhouse-Five*, Vonnegut remarks that there are "almost no characters in this story" because the war has made them "so sick" and so weak that they are merely "the listless playthings of enormous forces" (208). This is certainly a good description of Billy Pilgrim, the novel's protagonist, or main character. In fact, this description applies to Billy's entire life, not just his wartime experiences. Billy's extreme passivity makes him an unlikely hero for a war novel, but of course, this is actually an anti-war novel, and Billy is an anti-hero. Traditionally, a hero is smart, strong, and courageous. He makes things happen. An anti-hero is of average or below-average intelligence, weak, and fearful. Things happen to him, and he responds feebly. The tales of heroes give readers the impression that they can take charge of their own destiny. Stories about anti-heroes teach us about our limitations.

Billy Pilgrim's limitations are obvious from the beginning. As a child he is weak and "funny-looking," and as he grows he comes to resemble "a bottle of Coca-Cola" (30). He never learns to enjoy life, and it often seems that he would rather be dead. He has no strong preferences, so he is content to drift through life wherever the winds of chance may blow him. His physical limitations and lack of will make him a ridiculous soldier. Because he arrives at the front while his regiment is being destroyed, he is never properly equipped. Without a helmet or a single weapon, wearing cheap civilian shoes, he is more like an innocent bystander than a participant in the war. Billy's innocence and passivity help Vonnegut focus the reader's attention on the brutality of war. Because Billy Pilgrim never complains about any of the horrible things that happen to him, readers are moved to protest for him.

Several details in the novel suggest a connection between Billy Pilgrim and Jesus Christ. American literature is full of characters that can be considered "Christ figures," and it is tempting to include Billy Pilgrim on the list. When the Americans arrive at the first prison camp after ten days in the boxcar, Billy is hanging from the crossbeams, as if "self-crucified" (101). Late in life he has a brief career as the prophet of Tralfamadorian fatalism. Like Jesus during his last supper, he tells his followers that he must die soon, they protest, and he insists that his death is part of a larger plan. Like Jesus, Billy suffers and dies in spite of his innocence, and this is the most important connection between the two. In *Slaughterhouse-Five*, Billy and Jesus represent the suffering of essentially innocent people. But for Vonnegut, suffering does not come with the promise of a reward after death. It is simply a feature of human existence that can be relieved only by other human beings, not by supernatural intervention.

In an interview with Lee Roloff in 1996, Vonnegut revealed that Billy Pilgrim is based on an American prisoner, Edward Crone, whom he knew during the war. Like Billy, Crone was not physically fit to be a soldier, and he simply gave up trying to survive. He stared into space, refused to eat, and eventually died. In many ways, Billy Pilgrim is also dead, although he continues to breathe and things continue to happen to him. Whenever Vonnegut describes a corpse during the war, he mentions its "blue and ivory" feet (83, 188). Billy's feet are twice described as "blue and ivory," suggesting that he should also be considered a casualty of the war (35, 95). Billy's emotions are dead, and he is equally incapable of anger and joy. The happiest moment of his life is a nap in a "coffin-shaped" wagon a few days after the war has ended (248). On his wedding night, he thinks of the perfect words for his gravestone. Survivors of war are sometimes described as "walking wounded." Billy Pilgrim is a walking casualty of the Second World War, resuscitated by Vonnegut's imagination to give readers a glimpse of war's terrible human cost.

Eighteen-year-old Roland Weary, who takes up with Billy Pilgrim after the Battle of the Bulge, is in many ways Billy's opposite. While Billy is poorly equipped for battle and reluctant to fight, Weary carries everything the army ever gave him, along with some gruesome weapons of his own. As the most fully developed character among the soldiers that Billy meets, Weary is the prime example of how stories that glorify war shape the attitudes of young boys and make them eager to fight. Weary's father collects weapons and instruments of torture, and Roland shares his fascination. He carries with pride a gift from his father, a three-sided trench knife with spiked brass knuckles on the handle. He lectures Billy on tortures and execution. In spite of this, Vonnegut solicits the reader's sympathy for Weary by mentioning how unpopular he was as a boy. Because he was "stupid and fat and mean" the other children did not want him around, and he was always being "ditched" (44). His cruel fantasies are his refuge from a cruel world. He copes with the stress of battle by imagining that the war is already over and he is safe at home, telling the story of his adventures to his adoring family. He thinks of himself and the two scouts as the "Three Musketeers" who team up to save the hapless Billy Pilgrim. War stories and an overactive imagination have made him absurdly overconfident and inattentive to what is really going on around him. He is really a boy playing war, not a soldier. Of course, Weary's war "romance" does not come true. After the scouts leave them behind, he and Billy are captured by the Germans. Forced to exchange his combat boots for a pair of wooden clogs that cut his feet, Weary's "true war story" ends with his death from gangrene in a railroad car on the way to the prison camp (53).

Edgar Derby is more than twice Weary's age, and yet he is only slightly better prepared for war. A high-school civics teacher from Indianapolis, Derby had to pull political strings to get into the army at the age of forty-four. Like Weary, he is constantly turning his experiences into a mental narrative, but Derby does not glorify his exploits. Instead, he imagines comforting letters intended to reassure his wife that he will return home safely. These letters are poignant because Vonnegut reminds readers every time Derby appears that he is doomed to be executed for stealing a teapot from the ruins of Dresden. As a civics teacher who volunteered to fight against Nazism, Derby represents a naive, prewar faith in American values that Vonnegut once shared. When the American Nazi Howard W. Campbell, Jr., confronts the prisoners, only Derby summons the energy and will to denounce Campbell as a traitor to those values. He demonstrates his compassion for others by volunteering to watch over Billy during his stay in the hospital and by assuming the role of leader and attempting to get all of his men home safely. He is the most admirable character in the book, which makes his senseless death all the more lamentable.

The science fiction writer Kilgore Trout appears in several Vonnegut novels, and he is an important character in *Slaughterhouse-Five*. Although he has written many novels, none of them has sold well, so Trout makes a living by managing newspaper delivery boys in Ilium, New York. At sixty-two years old, with a full beard and a "paranoid face," he looks like a "prisoner of war"(212). Trout allows Vonnegut to express his frustration with the publishing industry, critics, and the American reading public, who ignored his work for so long (for more on Vonnegut's struggle to receive recognition as a writer, see chapters 1 and 2 of this volume). Like Vonnegut early in his career, Trout labors in obscurity, turning out stories and novels that few people read. Unlike Vonnegut, Trout deserves to be ignored because his writing is terrible; only his ideas are interesting. Trout is described as a "cracked messiah," and his novels include a rewrite of the New Testament and a parable about a money tree. Vonnegut includes quick summaries of three of Trout's novels, and they provide new perspectives on *Slaughterhouse-Five*'s major themes. They will be discussed more fully in the section on themes.

Bertram Copeland Rumfoord's name will also be familiar to avid Vonnegut readers. Other members of the incredibly wealthy Rumfoord family were major characters in Vonnegut's second novel, *The Sirens of Titan*. At seventy, B.C. Rumfoord is a Harvard professor, a retired general in the Air Force Reserve, and the author of twenty-six books, including one on "sex and strenuous athletics for men over sixty-five" (236). He has recently married his fifth wife, a twenty-three-year-old former "go-go-girl." Rumfoord considers himself a "superman," and he looks down on other human beings with contempt. Sharing a hospital room with Billy Pilgrim in Vermont, he says that Billy should be allowed to die from the head injuries he suffered in the plane crash. Like the Nazis, he believes that all weak people should die. Rumfoord exemplifies what Vonnegut calls the "military manner" of thinking and demonstrates how feeble are its justifications of mass murder (246). Because he finds Billy's presence in the room "inconvenient," he insists that Billy is suffering from a loathsome disease and therefore should die. The same twisted reasoning argues that because Germans were infected with Nazism, and the North Vietnamese with communism, they must be killed to prevent the spread of the disease. Billy has to struggle to prove that he is a human being worthy of respect. To Rumfoord's credit, he does eventually listen to Billy's account of the bombing of Dresden, but he stubbornly clings to the official justification that Dresden had to be bombed to hasten the end of the war.

Vonnegut has been criticized for failing to create believable female characters, and that criticism is justified in *Slaughterhouse-Five*, but only if we judge it by the standards of a conventional novel. Billy Pilgrim's wife Valencia is no more than a walking eating disorder who occasionally summons enough energy to say something stupid, but Vonnegut is not trying to draw a convincing portrait of a real woman. Instead, Valencia represents the spiritually empty consumerism that is typical of post-war American society. Not surprisingly, Montana Wildhack, the star of Billy's adolescent fantasy of guilt-free sexual obsession, remains two-dimensional, just like her picture in pornographic magazines. Although such flat, unsympathetic characters could be considered a weakness in a conventional narrative, they are appropriate in *Slaughterhouse-Five* because they help Vonnegut convey his vision of a superficial, sex-obsessed society.

THEMATIC ISSUES

One way of discussing the thematic issues in *Slaughterhouse-Five* is to consider the questions that Vonnegut asks in the novel. Having survived the fire bombing of Dresden, the major question he had to contend with was Why did this happen? The specific question of why Dresden was bombed leads to more general questions about why human beings wage war and what can be done to prevent wars in the future. As one of the few survivors of the greatest massacre in European history, Vonnegut also asks how people cope with the memories of a disaster and build new lives that make sense to them. In his typical fashion, Vonnegut explores these difficult questions and makes his readers think about them more deeply, without providing any definitive answers.

Although some readers find the science fiction aspects of *Slaughterhouse-Five* distracting, they provide an important perspective on the issue of why wars happen. If we could see the past and the future as clearly as we see the present, perhaps we could better understand the causes of war. Of course we cannot, so Vonnegut created creatures who can, in order to help us think about what this unique perspective on events could teach us. The Tralfamadorians tell Billy Pilgrim that their ability to see the past and the future has led them to conclude that all events are inevitable, so nothing they can do will change what must happen. For them the question "why?" is meaningless. But if we believe this, we are likely to give up trying and just shrug our shoulders and say "so it goes." Because Billy Pilgrim adopts this attitude, many readers believe that Vonnegut also endorses it, but a careful reading of the novel reveals that this is an oversimplification that distorts Vonnegut's complex vision. While it is true that the novel adopts the Tralfamadorian custom of saying "so it goes" every time a death occurs, this relentless repetition shows that the fatalistic attitude behind the saying is ridiculous. Eventually readers must rebel and insist that no, it did not have to go that way. Something could and should have been done to make things turn out differently. Death is inevitable, but some deaths are preventable, and the novel consistently demonstrates that human beings have the power to shape the present and the future. For example, during the hellish train trip to the prison camp, Billy Pilgrim glimpses a "heaven on wheels" that is part of the very same train (103). Four railroad guards share this cozy boxcar, and its simple furnishings reveal how easy it is for human beings to create a heaven for themselves on earth. Lit by candles and heated by a wood-burning stove, decorated with drawings of castles and lakes, the guard's car provides all of the comforts of a peasant's hut, including a simple meal of soup, bread, sausage, and wine. It seems like heaven to Billy because of the sharp contrast with his own uncomfortable situation, but by calling it "heaven" three times, Vonnegut is insisting that if human beings learned to be content with life's basic necessities, they could create a heaven for themselves right here on earth.

So, if wars are not inevitable and heaven on earth is possible, what prevents human beings from living in peace? While they are in the VA hospital, Eliot Rosewater gives Billy Pilgrim a brief summary of Kilgore Trout's novel *The Gospel from Outer Space* that provides an intriguing perspective on this difficult question. A visitor from another planet comes to earth and tries to figure out "why Christians found it so easy to be cruel," in spite of Jesus's message of peace and love (138). The alien decides that Christians are cruel because of faulty storytelling in the gospels. Because readers know that Jesus is the son of God from the beginning, they come to the conclusion that the Romans made a big mistake killing someone so "well connected" (139). This implies that it is all right to kill people who are not so well connected. Trout argues that the gospels teach Christians to discriminate between different kinds of people and to use discrimination to justify acts of cruelty. Whether or not we agree with Trout's analysis of the cause of discrimination, *Slaughterhouse-Five* shows that cruelty is often justified by denying the humanity of its victims. For example, the Nazis consider Russians less than human, so they condemn them to starve in an "extermination camp" while they pamper their English prisoners (102). Billy's first fleeting glimpse of a Russian affirms their common humanity, in spite of all the differences between them. The Russian looks "directly into Billy's soul with sweet hopefulness, as though Billy might have good news for him" (105). Of course, Billy does not have good news for him, but Vonnegut does have some good news for his readers: Even in the midst of war it is possible for two human beings to connect with each other, in spite of all the barriers that others have erected to keep them apart. On two separate occasions Vonnegut compares the face of a Russian prisoner to the luminous radium dial on a pocket watch (104, 115). In between these comparisons, he tells the story of Billy's childhood descent into the complete darkness of Carlsbad Caverns. Billy was terrified and "didn't even know whether he was alive or not," until his father pulled out his pocket watch and its radium dial provided a small source of light (114). The flicker of recognition that passes between Billy and the Russian prisoners is like that feeble light in total darkness, a small source of hope and an affirmation that all is not lost. If we are to avoid wars in the future, we must begin by recognizing that our common humanity is much more important than the social and cultural differences that divide us.

Although this insight provides some hope for the future, how can the survivors of past wars cope with their horrible memories and build new lives for themselves? Eliot Rosewater and Billy Pilgrim both end up in the VA hospital because after what they have seen in the war life no longer makes sense to them. Rosewater has become an alcoholic, but alcohol only dulls the pain, it does not cure his psychological wounds. He tells his psychiatrist that after the war people need "a lot of wonderful *new* lies" in order to make life seem worth living (129). From

Rosewater's perspective, religion, philosophy, and literature are old lies that no longer provide him with a sense of meaning and purpose. Convinced that life is meaningless, Rosewater does not expect to find a truth he can believe in, but he would like some comforting new lies to give him something to think about beside his painful memories. In his search for new lies, Rosewater turns to science fiction. The wacky ideas of Kilgore Trout appeal to him because they help him see life from many new perspectives, and because they are so crazy that he is never in danger of mistaking them for the truth. After his head injury, Billy Pilgrim does mistake Trout's lies for the truth. He believes that he has been kidnapped by Tralfamadorians and adopts their fatalistic view of life. Although the novel as a whole ridicules fatalism, it does provide Billy with a comforting fiction that sustains him for the rest of his life. Trout's *Gospel from Outer Space* becomes his Bible, and it comforts him. In this way Vonnegut demonstrates the importance of fiction in the world today. Whether you believe its lies or not, fiction provides comfort by creating the illusion of a world that makes sense.

A CULTURAL POETICS READING

Developed in the 1970s and 1980s, cultural poetics is a critical approach that attempts to read texts in their historical and cultural contexts (for an introduction to cultural poetics, see chapter 3 of this volume). In order to arrive at a reading of a text, a cultural poetics critic attempts to answer three basic questions: How are the author's experiences and beliefs reflected in the text? What are the rules and expectations of the culture in which the text was produced? How does the text add to the ongoing conversation about those rules? This cultural poetics reading of Kurt Vonnegut's *Slaughterhouse-Five* will attempt to answer these three questions.

In the first chapter, Vonnegut explains that *Slaughterhouse-Five* is based on his experiences during the war, and he reminds readers of this by interrupting the narrative with comments such as, "I was there" (86) and "That was I. That was me" (160, 189). In spite of these periodic first-person intrusions, Vonnegut is not really a character in the story, and he does not present his experiences directly. Readers should keep in mind that Billy Pilgrim is not Vonnegut, even though their wartime experiences are quite similar. Like Billy Pilgrim, Vonnegut had very little military training before being sent into combat. He was taken prisoner by the Germans during the Battle of the Bulge and brought to Dresden to work in a factory that made malt syrup for pregnant women. Like Billy, he survived the firebombing of the city and was forced to dig into the rubble to remove rotting corpses. Creating the character of Billy Pilgrim allows Vonnegut to present his experiences indirectly, as if they had happened to someone else, even as the autobiographical first chapter reminds readers that "[a]ll this happened, more or less" (1).

Vonnegut's fundamental beliefs were shaped during the 1920s and 1930s, tested by his wartime experiences, and refined in the 1960s as he wrote *Slaughterhouse-Five*. The horrible carnage of World War I led many Americans to believe that wars should be avoided at all cost. This idea, known as pacifism, was often coupled with isolationism, the notion that America could stay out of future wars by not making alliances with foreign nations. As a young man, Vonnegut was both a pacifist and an isolationist, arguing as late as 1941 that the United States should stay out of the war in Europe. His teachers taught him to be proud that he lived in a nation without a large standing army, where military men had no role in government, and where the people determined their own destiny through democratic institutions. The Japanese attack on Pearl Harbor convinced him that the United States must put aside pacifism and isolationism to defend democracy, but it did not undermine his basic belief that, except in extraordinary circumstances, wars should be avoided. Vonnegut's pacifism is clearly reflected in *Slaughterhouse-Five*. He shows that war makes soldiers lose sight of what they are fighting for as they struggle to survive. Democratic values are mentioned only once in the novel, as Edgar Derby denounces the American Nazi Howard W. Campbell, Jr. Derby, a high school civics teacher from Indianapolis, clearly speaks for the teachers who taught Vonnegut to love his country and its noble ideals of "freedom and justice and fair play for all" (209). The bombing of Dresden shook Vonnegut's faith in his country. How could a nation claim to stand for justice and fair play and then kill 135,000 civilians in a single night? After the war, when Vonnegut requested information on the Dresden raid from the Air Force, he was told that it was still "top secret," which made him wonder "Secret? . . . from *whom?*" (14). The obvious answer is that it was being kept secret from the American public, lest it damage their faith in the government and its armed forces. *Slaughterhouse-Five* demonstrates repeatedly that wars, and the "military manner" of thinking, make people betray the values that they claim to be defending (246).

After World War II the rules and expectations of American culture began to change. Americans did not return to pacifism and isolationism as they had after the First World War. As the only major nation to emerge from the war without serious damage to its industries, the United States assumed a position of power and influence in the world. Americans were told that now that they had defeated fascism, the only serious threat was from communism. The Soviet Union and China were the new enemies, and the cold war had begun. Rather than reducing the size of the armed forces, the government embarked on a massive military buildup. As he left office, President Dwight D. Eisenhower, who had commanded Allied forces in Europe during the Second World War, warned the nation of the unprecedented power of the "military-industrial complex" that came to dominate United States policy in the 1950s and 1960s. Unfortunately his warning was not heeded, and the alliance between arms manufacturers and the military kept the pressure on Congress to ensure that newer and more powerful weapons systems were developed. A clear shift in the nation's values was underway. The return of prosperity after the war and the introduction of new consumer products sent Americans on a spending spree. Middle class life was not complete unless a new Chrysler was parked in the driveway and the latest kitchen gadgets gleamed on the countertop. But the new products were more than mere conveniences. They were seen as concrete evidence of the superiority of the capitalist system over communism.

The pace of change accelerated in the 1960s. African Americans began to challenge racial segregation and the unwritten rules that denied them full participation in American society. Peaceful protest in the early 1960s was followed by race riots in major American cities in 1966 and 1967. Meanwhile, the war in Vietnam dragged on with no end in sight. In 1968, the majority of Americans still supported the war because they believed it was important to stop the spread of communism. But the apparent lack of progress, a major North Vietnamese offensive, and reports of American atrocities against Vietnamese civilians led more and more people to oppose the war.

Slaughterhouse-Five contributed to the national debate on all of these issues. By jumping around in time, Vonnegut forced his readers to consider how American values had changed during the course of the twentieth century. The pacifism and isolationism that Vonnegut absorbed in the 1930s appealed to a new generation who had become disillusioned with the militant anticommunism of the 1950s and early 1960s. Vonnegut's experience as a victim of an American bombing raid made him especially well qualified to speak out against the civilian casualties caused by American bombers in Vietnam. By showing readers what it was like to be on the receiving end of American military might, he demonstrated the folly of killing people to save them from communism.

Scenes from Billy Pilgrim's life after the war provide Vonnegut with an opportunity to comment on some of the major issues in American society in the 1960s. Billy's materially prosperous but spiritually empty life demonstrates that consumerism is no replacement for the fundamental values that many Americans abandoned after the war. His brief glimpse of the burned-out Ilium ghetto reminds white Americans that the ideal of "freedom and justice and fair play for all" has never applied to African Americans (209). *Slaughterhouse-Five* is a book about World War II, but it is also a book about America in the 1960s. It is both a product of its times and an astute commentary on them.

Bluebeard
(1987)

Kurt Vonnegut celebrated forty years as a professional writer with the publication of *Bluebeard*, the best of his later novels. In *Bluebeard* Vonnegut revisits the major themes of his earlier novels, including the question of personal identity, the role of the artist in society, the importance of family, the American class system, and the physical and emotional costs of war. However, *Bluebeard* is more than just an encore by an acclaimed performer. Like a seasoned jazz musician, Vonnegut plays variations on his favorite themes and then ventures into new territory. *Bluebeard* is the first of Vonnegut's novels to take a serious look at relationships between men and women. For the first time in his fiction, strong female characters seem to speak for themselves, rather than being mere tokens for the author's ideas. Two well-developed female characters give *Bluebeard* a new dimension that earlier novels lacked.

Bluebeard is presented as the autobiography of Rabo Karabekian, a minor Abstract Expressionist artist whose most famous works fell apart because he used defective paint. Almost all of the novel's major characters are artists, and Vonnegut reflects on the importance of art to society and to the individuals who create it. Vonnegut shows his readers the joy that artists experience when the creative fervor is upon them and also points out the price that their families pay for their dedication to their work. His extended discussion of the relative merits of realism and expressionism in the visual arts sheds light upon the craft of the novelist as well. Putting aside the science fiction elements that he used so suc-

cessfully in earlier novels, Vonnegut revisits his major themes in a realistic mode and reaffirms the fundamental importance of telling a good
story. *Bluebeard* is a virtuoso performance, and a close reading of the
novel provides an opportunity to assess Vonnegut's achievement as a
novelist.

PLOT DEVELOPMENT

Written in the first person, *Bluebeard* claims to be the autobiography
of Rabo Karabekian, son of Armenian immigrant parents, illustrator,
World War II veteran, Abstract Expressionist artist, art collector, and
"one-eyed man" (1). But as Karabekian points out on the first page, the
book is also about the summer of 1987 when it was written. *Bluebeard*
mingles recollections of the 1930s, 1940s, and 1950s with periodic up-
dates from the summer of 1987 to comment on how much has changed
in America since Karabekian's birth in 1916. Karabekian begins by telling
his parents' story. At the beginning of the twentieth century, they survived the almost total annihilation of the Armenian people by the Turks
and came to America to start over. In the old country, Karabekian's father was a respected teacher of the Armenian language and literature,
and he dreamed of teaching in an Armenian school in the United States.
He escaped the Turkish soldiers who raided his village by hiding in the
school's latrine, covered in filth. Karabekian's mother lived in another
village and escaped death when she was taken to "the killing fields" by
pretending to be dead and hiding under corpses (4). Under a pile of
bodies, she found herself staring into the face of an old woman. The
jewels the old woman had hidden from the Turks were spilling out of
her mouth. When nightfall came and Karabekian's mother could escape,
she scooped up the jewels and took them with her to Persia, where she
met her future husband. From there they went to Egypt, selling jewels
as needed to meet their expenses. In Egypt they met another survivor of
the Armenian genocide, Vartan Mamigonian, who sold them a false
dream that was too good to resist. He told them that an Armenian community in San Ignacio, California, was desperate for a new teacher, so
they would sell him a beautiful house and fertile land for a fraction of
its true value. Karabekian's parents sold most of the jewels for a photograph of a house and a worthless deed. When they arrived in San
Ignacio they discovered that there was no house and no Armenian community. But rather than move to one of the Armenian communities in
California, Karabekian's father decided to stay in San Ignacio and take

up his father's trade, shoe repair. As he looks back, Karabekian decides that his father cheated himself much more effectively than Mamigonian cheated him. He never learned to speak English well, and he did not take advantage of any of the opportunities that life in America offered him because he preferred to wallow in his bitterness.

Karabekian explains that he is writing his autobiography at the insistence of a new acquaintance and houseguest, Circe Berman, whom he met one fine June day on the beach in front of his mansion on Long Island. Berman's first words to Karabekian are, "Tell me how your parents died," and this unexpected conversation starter sets the tone of their relationship (14). Berman always keeps Karabekian off balance, and she gets him thinking about aspects of his life that he would rather forget. After telling her how his mother died from a tetanus infection she picked up while working in a cannery in California when he was twelve, and how his father died while watching a movie ten years later, Karabekian begins to recall his father's bitterness. Cut off from the people and the culture he loved, Karabekian's father pities himself relentlessly, while at the same time refusing to do anything to improve his life. Berman tries to help Karabekian understand his father by explaining that he suffered from "Survivors' Syndrome" (22). People who survive massacres sometimes feel that they should have died along with all the others, so they suffer from feelings of guilt and shame. According to this theory, his futile life was his way of punishing himself for having survived.

After this long conversation on the beach, Karabekian invites Circe Berman to supper and eventually to stay at his house, in spite of all the discomfort that her persistent questions cause him. She criticizes his priceless art collection, which also happens to be the work of his closest friends. She announces that she will take over meal planning because Karabekian and his friend, novelist Paul Slazinger, seem to be suffering from the debilitating effects of a diet too rich in cholesterol. She annoys Slazinger, who suffers from writer's block, by declaring that she is on Long Island to work on a biography of her late husband, a well-known brain surgeon. Slazinger resents the implication that anyone can be a writer and decides to let her know just how tough writing can be. But as Karabekian soon reveals to the reader, the joke is on Slazinger. Circe Berman is no amateur writer. She is the author of the highly successful "Polly Madison" books for young readers, which have sold millions of copies and been made into movies. She has an opinion on every subject and a good argument to back it up. Furthermore, she delights in assigning people projects that she believes will do them good, so she gets Karabekian to start writing his autobiography. As the initiator of the project, she feels entitled to barge in on him at any time and take a look at what he has written. The first half of the book is punctuated by Berman's comments on Karabekian's writing.

Berman also feels free to snoop around Karabekian's house to learn more about him, but there is a potato barn on the property that he keeps locked up. He tells everyone that it is not to be opened until after his death, and of course this arouses Berman's insatiable curiosity. She begins by demanding entry, and when she is refused admission, she begins guessing, and Karabekian starts dropping hints. He calls himself "Bluebeard" after the old children's story of the brutal husband who kept one room in his castle off-limits to his wives. When he catches his wife looking into the room, he kills her and adds her body to those of her predecessors in the forbidden room. Karabekian quickly assures readers that there are no bodies in his barn, but he keeps the contents secret until the end of the book. However, at one time the barn was his studio, and his ongoing obsession with art and his own place in art history indicates that the barn probably contains a painting.

As a child in San Ignacio, California, Karabekian discovers that he is good at drawing and dreams of becoming an artist. His parents discourage him because, as everyone knows, artists never make money during their lifetimes. Then one day his mother reads a magazine article about a fabulously wealthy magazine and book illustrator named Dan Gregory, who just happens to be a fellow Armenian. She encourages Karabekian to write him a letter praising his work, mentioning the Armenian connection, and expressing a wish to become "an artist half as good as he is" (55). Although Gregory pays no attention to the letter, it does catch the interest of Marilee Kemp, Gregory's mistress. Marilee is a twenty-one-year-old former "showgirl," who grew up in the coal-mining region of West Virginia (55). Although she calls herself Gregory's "assistant," she is not really involved in his business (56). Gregory does not even take her out or introduce her to his famous friends. In her letters to Karabekian, she discovers that she has a talent for writing. She begins describing scenes of New York life, supposedly so that he can paint them, but really to practice her craft. Karabekian saves all her letters and eventually has them bound in a handsome volume that he keeps in his library. When Circe Berman reads them she points out how Marilee found her own distinctive voice by writing for an "audience of one," claiming that one reader is really all a writer needs, an opinion that Vonnegut has endorsed in interviews (65). Marilee sends Karabekian the finest art supplies, taken from Gregory's supply room without his knowledge, and he sends her his finished works, realistic illustrations in Gregory's style.

By 1933, Karabekian is seventeen, his mother is dead, and he is living with his increasingly bitter father, who lost his life savings in a bank failure caused by the Great Depression. Karabekian treasures Marilee's letters as if they were tickets to a better life, and one day, a train ticket to New York actually arrives, along with a telegram from Gregory, inviting Karabekian to come and be his apprentice. It seems that his late mother's dream for him is about to come true, but as Karabekian learns years later, her dream is fulfilled because another woman is living a nightmare. When Marilee finally dares to show Gregory some of Karabekian's work, he flies into a rage because he recognizes his own art supplies and realizes that Marilee must have stolen them. He pushes her down the stairs, and she breaks both legs and one arm. Visiting her in the hospital, Gregory is remorseful, promises her anything if she will forgive him, and she asks for Karabekian to come and be Gregory's apprentice. By the time Karabekian arrives, however, Gregory has recovered from his feelings of guilt, and he does everything he can think of to show Karabekian that he is unwelcome. To explain the harsh treatment, Gregory describes his own apprenticeship in Moscow to the engraver who made the plates for printing the Imperial currency. The story is a perfect little folk tale that illuminates some of the novel's central themes. Jealous of the young Gregory's talent, the engraver sets him a task that everyone in the shop agrees is impossible: to draw a one ruble note accurately enough to fool a merchant in the marketplace. Gregory spends six months working on his counterfeit, but when he displays it, the engraver just laughs and tears it to pieces. Gregory spends another six months creating an even better counterfeit, but this, too, his master rejects. Finally he works for a year on a copy that he considers perfect, but rather than show it to his master, he presents him with the real note that he used as a model. Believing it to be a fake, the engraver scorns it once again, but Gregory snatches it from his hand and runs to the market, where he uses it to buy a box of cigars. When he returns, the engraver is terrified, because the penalty for counterfeiting is death, and he is sure that the false ruble will be traced back to his shop. He asks Gregory for the real note, which is, of course, the fake, and rushes out to exchange it for the ruble that Gregory spent. When he returns, it is Gregory's turn to laugh. He tells his master that this stunt proves he is a "genius" because he fooled the engraver into passing a counterfeit ruble (112). Gregory credits his subsequent success as an artist to the harsh treatment he endured as an apprentice and the nearly impossible challenge he was given, so he decides to do the same for Karabekian. He assigns him to paint a perfect image of his studio, an enormous room filled with many curious objects that Gregory has painted over the years. To achieve the level of accuracy that his master requires, Karabekian has to learn the names and functions of every part of every object in the room and use a magnifying glass to paint details that the unaided eye cannot see.

At this point, Karabekian interrupts his autobiography to report on events from the summer of 1987. Circe Berman decides that he needs to go to New York City to prove to himself that he is still alive and capable of action. But while he is away, visiting places familiar from his youth, she redecorates part of his house. When he returns, his valuable Abstract Expressionist paintings have been replaced by Victorian "chromos" of little girls on swings. The "stark-white" walls have been covered in bright, floral wallpaper (124). Karabekian is furious. Berman says that she has tried to appreciate his abstract paintings, so he should try to understand her preference for the realistic portraits of little girls. She asks him to think about why people in the last century admired these pictures so much. When they looked at the innocence of the little girls, the Victorians thought of the horrors that awaited most of them in a few more years: "diphtheria, pneumonia, smallpox, miscarriages, violent husbands, poverty, widowhood, prostitution—death and burial in a potter's field" (138). For Berman, this story of harsh experience lurking beneath the surface innocence of the paintings makes them "twice as serious" as modern abstract paintings, which are "about absolutely nothing" (137, 39).

After the fight over the paintings, Berman is planning to leave, and Karabekian's cook, his only remaining servant, gives her two-week notice as well. Looking at life alone in his great big house, Karabekian is scared, and he asks the cook to explain why she is leaving him. Although he pays her well, he refers to her as "the cook," never bothering to use her name, which makes her feel like "a nobody and a nothing" (140). Karabekian admits that he used to hear a similar complaint from his first wife, when he neglected her to concentrate on his painting. The cook, also known as Allison White, forces him to admit that he is scared of women. Although he tries to remember to use her name in the rest of the book, the frequency with which he forgets reveals that the reeducation of Rabo Karabekian will be a long process. When Circe Berman returns from a dinner party, she wakes him up to tell him that

Allison White will stay if she does, and Karabekian returns to writing his autobiography.

Karabekian recalls how Dan Gregory made him repeat the phrase "The Emperor has no clothes" every time modern art was mentioned (146). From Gregory's point of view, abstract art is "the work of swindlers and lunatics and degenerates," who splatter paint on canvas because they are incapable of painting realistically (147). He forbids Marilee and Karabekian to enter the Museum of Modern Art as a way of proving their loyalty to him. Karabekian puts up with Gregory's abusive treatment and his whims because it is the 1930s, and he does not want to give up free food and shelter in the middle of the Great Depression. He and Marilee become close friends on long walks around the city, and soon they are attracted to the forbidden museum. On Saint Patrick's Day 1936, Gregory's open car is stuck in traffic, and he spots Karabekian and Marilee coming out of the Museum of Modern Art. Karabekian compares the moment to the expulsion of Adam and Eve from the Garden of Eden and to Bluebeard's wife peering in the forbidden closet. He and Marilee are banished from the paradise of Gregory's mansion and told to fend for themselves on the mean streets of Depression-era New York. But before they go, they make love. It is Karabekian's first time, and he imagines that they are promising to be loyal to each other forever, but afterwards, Marilee explains that she will return to Gregory. She points out that in real life, unlike the opera, sensible women do not leave successful men for romantic boys. After his departure, Karabekian dreams of becoming a great artist and taking Marilee away from Gregory, but the Depression soon teaches him that such events are more frequent in stories than in real life. For months, he survives in soup kitchens and homeless shelters, picking up a little money drawing caricatures of people in Central Park. There he meets Marc Coloumb, a young Armenian businessman in New York to promote his family's successful travel agency. Coloumb admires Karabekian's talent, buys him a suit, and arranges for an advertising agency to hire him. With a steady income, he decides to take art lessons and applies to the Art Students League. The teacher takes one look at the cameralike realism of his paintings and declares that, although "technically speaking" they are flawless, they show such a lack of "passion" that Karabekian will never be a great artist (201–2).

Paul Slazinger, Karabekian's novelist friend who had been looking into the plight of repressed artists in communist Poland, makes a dramatic return to the novel at the end of chapter 23. At about midnight, the local rescue squad delivers him to Karabekian's door in a straightjacket. He had awakened his neighbors by screaming for help from the windows of his house. When the rescue squad arrived, he said he would be all right if they would take him to Karabekian's house. His sudden arrival brings Circe Berman downstairs in a state that Karabekian describes as "almost catatonic" (206). Although she usually takes control of every situation, one look at the crazed Slazinger makes her retreat to her bedroom. After putting Slazinger to bed, Karabekian stops at her room to ask for a sleeping pill for his friend and finds her "staring straight ahead" (207). When he enters her bathroom to look for the pills, countless bottles line the counter. Apparently Circe Berman is a "pill freak," and Karabekian uses this new information to explain her strange behavior (207). When he wakes up the next day, Salzinger is calm but still crazy. He raves about the Polly Madison books, which he has spent the summer reading, and vows to secure for them their rightful place in the canon of serious literature. He also begins his first work of nonfiction, an explanation of why revolutions succeed or fail. With Berman and Slazinger both hard at work on their writing, Karabekian decides it is time to return to his autobiography.

When World War II began in Europe, Marc Coloumb's travel agency went out of business and Karabekian lost his job, so he joined the U.S. Army. Because the United States had not entered the war yet, the army was small, and Karabekian describes it as a "little family" he was happy to join (216). Assigned to paint the portrait of a general who was about to retire, Karabekian convinces him to create a camouflage unit made up of artists and to put him in charge. So Karabekian spends the war with a "happy family" of thirty-six artists, traveling all over Europe and North Africa creating illusions for the Nazis to photograph from the air (2). Near the end of the war, he finally sees action in the Battle of the Bulge, a massive German counterattack, and loses one eye. Recovering in an army hospital, he meets his first wife, Dorothy, a nurse. Looking back, Karabekian has trouble explaining his decision to marry, since he "had so few gifts as a husband and a father," and he finds himself saying, "That's the way the postwar movie goes" (223). Karabekian's postwar movie features rapid estrangement from his wife and two sons, whom he neglects in order to spend time drinking with his painter friends. His closest friend is Terry Kitchen, the talented son of wealthy parents who decides to paint because it is one activity that does not come easily to him. Their circle of friends includes Jackson Pollock, the best known of the Abstract Expressionist artists of the postwar years. Karabekian is popular with the group because he always has enough money to pay for drinks, thanks to his army pension and some investments in the stock market. His artist friends pay him back with paintings that are worthless at the time but that become quite valuable years later. In 1950 Karabekian's aimless life is interrupted by a telegram summoning him to Italy to testify in a court case about art treasures that had been looted by the Germans during the war. While he is in Florence, he receives a note from Marilee, who is now the Contessa Portomaggiore. Back in the late 1930s she came to Italy with Dan Gregory, who was a great admirer of Mussolini. The Italian dictator was happy to have a famous American painter and his beautiful mistress in his entourage, and soon Marilee was being introduced as an "actress" and a celebrity in her own right (242). After Gregory was killed by British troops in Egypt, while wearing an Italian uniform, Marilee was revered by the Italian people. She was escorted around Rome by Mussolini's minister of culture, Count Bruno Portomaggiore. Count Bruno told her immediately that their relationship could never be sexual, because he was attracted only to men, but for the first time in her life Marilee had a man who treated her with respect. When rumors circulated that the count was a homosexual and a spy for the British, Mussolini demanded that he marry Marilee. At first she refused, but an American agent visited her and asked her to marry Bruno and become a spy for the United States. When her husband was executed for spying, she inherited his estate and staffed it with women who were injured during the war.

When Karabekian arrives at her palazzo, he expects to resume the romance they began fourteen years earlier, but Marilee has a big surprise for him. She mocks him by saying, "Thought you were going to get laid again, I bet," and she reveals how she has suffered her entire life at the hands of men who claimed that they loved her (234). She finally tells Karabekian that Gregory only agreed to hire him because he was sorry he had pushed her down the stairs. In an earlier telephone conversation, Karabekian mentioned that he had many women during the war. Now Marilee uses his boast to humiliate him by pointing out that during the war, women "would do anything for food or protection for themselves" and their loved ones (238). She claims that humiliating women is the whole idea behind war. "It's always men against women, with the men only pretending to fight among themselves" (238). She goes on to compare Karabekian's injury to those suffered by her servant Lucrezia, who lost an eye and a leg to a land mine while delivering a couple of eggs to a neighbor who had just given birth.

Unfortunately, Marilee's lesson on the pain that men inflict on women does not help Karabekian to be a better husband when he returns to Dorothy. He forces her to move to a house on Long Island where he has rented a studio and continues to ignore her as he begins covering enormous canvases with Sateen Dura Luxe, a new brand of house paint guaranteed to "outlive the smile on the Mona Lisa" (21). In 1956 Dorothy finally leaves him, taking their two boys. A few weeks earlier his best friends, Terry Kitchen and Jackson Pollock, committed suicide, and their deaths, coupled with his wife's departure, make him feel like his father must have after the Turks destroyed his village. He retreats to his potato-barn studio and "lives like an animal . . . friendless and unloved" for eight years until he is "tamed" by the woman who owns the barn (284, 275). Edith Taft Fairbanks inherited the mansion where Karabekian now lives and shared it for many years with her first husband. After his death, she befriends and then marries Karabekian, redecorating her Victorian mansion to accommodate his valuable collection of modern art. Karabekian describes Edith as an "Earth Mother" who fills their home with life (7). Her death after twenty happy years of marriage leaves him feeling just as empty as he did when his first wife left him. He has not painted in many years, but now he returns to the potato barn to contemplate a blank canvas sixty-four feet long and eight feet high, composed of eight joined panels. It once held his largest, if not his greatest work, "Windsor Blue Number Seventeen," which adorned the lobby of the GEFFCo building in New York until the paint began to peel away. Karabekian cleaned the canvas panels and set them up in his abandoned studio "in their restored virginity" as a symbol of his desire to repair "all the damage I had done to myself and others in my brief career as a painter" (291). He calls the blank canvas "I Tried and Failed and Cleaned Up Afterward, so its *Your* Turn Now," and he plans to leave it blank, but after Edith's unexpected death he has the urge to create one more painting. Three years later, Circe Berman finally persuades him to open the barn and show her his final work. The painting shows a valley in Europe the morning World War II ended, as Karabekian saw it after being released from a German prison camp. Five-thousand-two-hundred-nineteen people from all over the world are depicted in precise detail, and Karabekian claims that he made up a complete story for each one. Circe Berman is overwhelmed by the painting's power, and she convinces Karabekian to put it on public display. He is concerned about what the critics will say, so he deprecates the painting's value as art, calling it a "watchamacallit" and a "tourist attraction" rather than a serious work (299). Yet he is thrilled that at last he has created something that seems to capture the public imagination, and he ends his book by exclaiming, "O happy Rabo Karabekian" (318).

CHARACTER DEVELOPMENT

Rabo Karabekian is a memorable addition to Vonnegut's roster of first-person narrators who reveal their characters as they tell their stories. Although readers cannot always take what they say about themselves at face value, these first-person narrators eventually reveal themselves in more subtle ways, through their choice of words, their obsessions, and the way they describe other characters. Like Howard W. Campbell, Jr., in *Mother Night* (see chapter 5 of this volume), Karabekian is on the defensive as he writes his memoirs. He is not on trial, but he feels the need to justify a life that has included many failures. He craves the approval of his few acquaintances and worries about what his reputation will be after he dies.

Karabekian does not have a strong personality of his own, so he creates identities for himself by following role models. Only at the end of his life does he begin to realize how poor his choices of role models have been. In his youth, he not only emulates Dan Gregory's artistic style, he adopts his racist and misogynistic attitudes as well. If he had not been thrown out of his master's house, he probably would have come to share Gregory's admiration for Mussolini. After the war, Karabekian once again falls under the sway of a poor role model, the alcoholic painter, Terry Kitchen. He adopts Kitchen's careless attitude toward everything but painting and it costs him his family. When Kitchen and Jackson Pollock commit suicide within a week of each other, Karabekian spends eight years living as a hermit before a caring woman provides him with a new role model, her recently deceased husband, who had been "a useless, harmless waster of life" (275). Because Edith has enough life for both of them, Karabekian is reasonably contented to waste his life at her side, but her death shows him how empty his life has become.

Although he claims that loneliness does not bother him, his sudden bursts of temper when he recalls close friends and family members who no longer speak to him—"Who gives a damn!"—reveal that he is deeply hurt (7). The loneliness he feels at seventy-one reminds him of his lonely youth as the only Armenian child in a small California town. Like so many of Vonnegut's characters, Karabekian is crippled emotionally by parents who never showed him the affection he needed as a child. Later in life he uses women to relieve his loneliness, but unable to show them real affection in return, his relationships are doomed to failure. The single exception, his happy marriage to Edith, actually proves this point. As an "Earth Mother" whose greatest joy comes from caring for crippled animals, she provides Karabekian with all the affection he needs and asks for nothing in return. She is the perfect replacement for his own mother, who died when he was eleven. His failure to call the cook by name shows his tendency to think of people solely in terms of how they can help him, rather than as full-fledged human beings with desires and needs of their own. His art also suffers from his failure to look beyond the surface appearance of things. Although he can capture the likeness of anything, his pictures lack "soul" because his own soul is so profoundly lacking in compassion and understanding for others. He dwells on the loss of his eye, but his preoccupation reveals more than simple vanity about his appearance. His loss of an eye is symbolic of his inability to see the people around him. With only one eye, his vision lacks depth and dimension, and his view of the world is as flat as the canvases he paints on. Yet in spite of his failures as a husband, father, and artist, the book apparently ends with a wiser Karabekian who has made peace with the past by admitting his failures. In his last painting, he finally finds a subject about which he has something to say. He has learned Marilee's lesson about war's terrible human cost, and he understands that every human being has a story to tell. By giving each of the people in his painting a unique story, he endows them with the soul that was lacking in his previous efforts. At the start of the book, he describes himself as a "museum guard," forgotten and irrelevant, waiting to die in a museum with no visitors (8). At the end of the book, he is still a museum guard, but now he greets a constant flow of visitors and enjoys watching them marvel at a painting he created.

However, in spite of what appears to be a happy ending, the book may actually be a long suicide note. Karabekian often thinks about the suicides of his close friends, Terry Kitchen and Jackson Pollock. He mentions that most artists are not appreciated during their lifetimes, and adds that if you really want to increase the value of the paintings you leave behind, you should consider suicide. Confronted with the possibility that he will have to live alone, Karabekian admits that he needs "someone as vivid" as Circe Berman to keep him alive, and as he finishes the book, she has been gone for two weeks (146). He says that the message of the painting in the potato barn is "Good-bye" (211). He recalls Marilee's conviction that the play *A Doll's House* should end with Nora's suicide, and that Ibsen "just tacked" on an upbeat ending "so the audience could go home *happy*"(159). Karabekian uses the word "happy" three times in the book's final paragraph, an obvious warning that this "happy" ending may be a fake. Finally, the title page reads: *Bluebeard: The Autobiography of Rabo Karabekian (1916–1988)* indicating that Karabekian died shortly after completing the book. Like *Mother Night*, *Bluebeard* can be read as a long suicide note that attempts to explain a life gone wrong.

Circe Berman is one of the few memorable female characters in Vonnegut's fiction. Her unusual first name recalls the beautiful enchantress in Homer's *Odyssey*, and early in their relationship, Rabo wonders if Mrs. Berman might be a "witch" (14). In the *Odyssey*, Circe turns Odysseus' men into pigs, and then at his insistence, she changes them back into men. Circe Berman works similar magic on Rabo Karabekian. At first she draws out his pigheaded side by criticizing his art collection and his way of life. Then her subtle humanizing influence begins to work on Karabekian as he puts his life in perspective by writing his autobiography. By the end of the book, she has turned Karabekian into a man who is worthy of being her friend. But Circe Berman is more than just a mysterious woman who works magic on Vonnegut's protagonist. She is a well-developed character in her own right, and this is what sets her apart from most of the other women in Vonnegut's fiction.

Circe Berman is a forty-something widow from Baltimore, who lost her husband Abe six months before meeting Karabekian on the beach. She has no children, and the death of her husband has left her lonely, but unlike Karabekian she will not be content with superficial friendship. When he says hello to her on the beach, she rejects the formulaic greeting and explains that "hello" is just a way of pretending to speak to someone when you really want to be left alone. Circe needs Karabekian just as much as he needs her, but he does not recognize her need. Making Karabekian into a fully functioning human being helps her to cope with the loss of her husband. Encouraging him to talk about his painful past, she says, "Tell Mama how your parents died," indicating that she will play the role of surrogate mother for Karabekian if he will allow it (15).

Circe Berman has an insatiable curiosity about other people and life in general ("I need information the way I need vitamins and minerals") and she puts this information to good use in her popular novels for young people (25). Her books are about real life right now, and millions of young readers have decided that they can trust her insights. Her confidence in her own work ("I am very proud of my titles") stands in sharp contrast to Karabekian's insecurity about his art (38). Her impressive knowledge of human psychology helps Karabekian come to grips with his father's bitterness and his own problems relating to women. But her confident exterior masks a troubled person still haunted by memories of her father's suicide when she was a teenager. Her writing allows her to concentrate on other people's troubles rather than becoming obsessed with her own. She has a pool table installed in Karabekian's house and explains her great skill by saying that after her father's suicide she played pool for ten hours a day. Now she uses the game to help her cope with the loss of her husband. When Karabekian discovers a "regiment" of pill bottles in her bathroom, he is quick to label her a "pill freak," but this says more about his desire to pigeonhole people than it does about Circe's real nature. Even if she is addicted to pills, her intelligence, compassion, and respect for others does not come from a bottle, and these qualities make her a memorable character.

Marilee Kemp is also a strong woman, and the novel gives a more complete picture of how her character developed. Raised by an illiterate, abusive coal miner in the mountains of West Virginia, she becomes an accomplished writer, marries an Italian count, and through her intelligence and hard work, she ends her days as the largest Sony distributor in Europe. It is the classic American "rags to riches" story, except that it plays out in Europe rather than in the United States. Marilee's beauty attracts a string of abusive men, from the high school football team that rapes her, to Dan Gregory, the famous artist who keeps her as a "pet" and beats her regularly (56). She discovers her talent for writing in her letters to Karabekian, and this proof of her intelligence changes her life. When Karabekian meets her in New York, she is still Gregory's pet, but she is determined not to be a victim any longer. She understands that Depression-era New York affords little opportunity for her to escape Gregory, but when she begins to receive favorable attention in Italy she uses it to her advantage. Mussolini's desire for a great propaganda victory turns her into a "famous actress" and brings her all the respect and admiration that a real actress could hope for (243). In public at least, Dan Gregory also has to treat her with respect, and Marilee enjoys this new feeling of power over a man who had abused her for so long. She soon speaks better Italian than Gregory does, and she uses this to her advantage. After his death, she becomes "the toast of Rome," and she finally meets a man who treats her well (245). After he is shot for being a spy, she expects to feel "a terrible emptiness," but she does not (250). Instead, she realizes that the true love of her life is the Italian people. She has finally found a home, thousands of miles from her birthplace. In a beautiful palazzo near Florence, she lives in the company of women who were injured during the war, savors the bitter wisdom that comes from a hard life, and yet somehow she preserves her sense of humor. Looking back at the botched abortion that Gregory forced her to have in Switzerland and that left her infertile, she jokes that she "should have thanked Dan for that" because the trip sparked her interest in foreign languages (58). She sees right through the nationalistic propaganda that men use to justify war, declaring that "it's always men against women, with the men only pretending to fight among themselves" (238). No longer a victim, she looks down on her former abusers with contempt, "believing that men were not only useless and idiotic, but downright dangerous" (244). Vonnegut has commented on the senseless brutality of war in most of his previous novels. Marilee Kemp takes his condemnation of war to a new level by pointing out that it is another way for men to oppress women.

THEMATIC ISSUES

Bluebeard is first and foremost a book about artists and the role of art in contemporary American society. *Bluebeard* affirms the fundamental human need to play and create. Early in the book, Karabekian muses that in the distant past, when people lived in small family groups, it was good to have someone who could tell stories, someone who could sing, someone else who could paint the walls of the cave, and so on. These "moderately gifted" people were valued by their communities and encouraged in their efforts (82). But today, modern communications technology makes it possible to listen to the world's best singers and storytellers and see the works of the best painters. The Author's Note that precedes the novel laments the "grotesque prices paid for art in the last century," and the novel shows how the commercialization of "human playfulness" has distorted the process of artistic creation. People with moderate artistic talent soon give up, since they cannot compete with the best. Just as the automated lathe put machinists out of work in Vonnegut's first novel, *Player Piano*, so the new communications technology makes local artists obsolete. Deprived of their creative outlet, these frustrated artists have to settle for unrewarding lives in a culture that affords few opportunities for creative self-expression. When he gives up his dream of becoming an artist, Karabekian discovers that his only option is to settle for "a more common and general sort of achievement than serious art, which was money" (48).

Bluebeard also addresses the issue of why some art is considered "serious" and other art is not. Most people take a work of art seriously only after being informed of its monetary value. When Terry Kitchen gave Karabekian one of his paintings in the 1950s, it was not serious art because no one wanted it. But after his suicide attracted the attention of art experts and made his work worth millions of dollars, it was a very

serious painting indeed. Most people are afraid to trust their own judgments about art because they believe that evaluating art takes years of
specialized training. Unlike Circe Berman, who knows what paintings
she likes and can explain why, they are intimidated by experts and need
to be told what to admire. According to the alleged art experts, any work
that has wide popular appeal cannot be taken seriously because the taste
of the general public is so poor that anything they like must be bad.
When Circe Berman redecorates Karabekian's foyer, "serious" and "popular" art come together, revealing very different assumptions about the
role of art in human life. Karabekian's paintings are one-of-a kind objects
whose value depends on the judgment of art experts and on their rarity.
Circe Berman's "chromos" of little girls on swings are prints that were
mass-produced using a process known as chromolithography. Their popularity in the nineteenth century puts them beneath the notice of art
experts, who consider them "kitsch," tasteless ornaments designed to
appeal to the uneducated masses. Mrs. Berman takes them seriously because she sees them in their social context. She knows that the Victorians
loved the innocence of these images because they knew that before long
these girls would experience illness, poverty, and the brutality of their
husbands. The pictures speak to her because she reads the story behind
them. Karabekian's pictures, on the other hand, are not designed to communicate. One thing that Berman and Karabekian can agree on is that
these paintings are "about nothing but themselves" (254). Even the titles—"Opus Nine," "Blue and Burnt Orange"—are intended to be "un-
communicative" (38). Although Karebekian is ashamed of his urge to tell
a story in his "serious" paintings, he finds it impossible not to tell himself
a secret story as he works, transforming his colored tapes into the souls
of people and animals. For Circe Berman, the whole purpose of art, indeed of life itself, is to communicate with others. Judging by the popular
success of Dan Gregory's pictures, which always told a story, most people would agree with her, if they were not so intimidated by the whole
subject of art. *Bluebeard* encourages readers to trust their own judgments
about art whether they agree with the so-called experts or not.

Circe Berman tells stories that help young people make sense of their
lives, and the importance of storytelling is one of *Bluebeard*'s major
themes. As a young man, Karabekian sees the world through the adventure stories he read as a child. They taught him that hard work and
virtue are always rewarded and that a poor boy with a dream can
achieve anything. Life on his own in Depression-era New York soon
teaches him otherwise, but he continues to try to live his life according
to someone else's script. He admits that he married his first wife because

"that's the way the postwar movie goes" (223). Circe Berman realizes that Karabekian needs to tell his own story because only by putting his experiences in writing can he make sense of his life. Writing his autobiography is a form of psychological therapy, and Karabekian learns something about himself on almost every page. Telling stories also allows powerless people to gain some degree of control over their own lives, as Marilee discovers when she starts writing letters to Karabekian. By the time he visits her in Florence, she is a master storyteller. Her account of her wartime experiences makes him respectful and envious of her eventful life. Writing also provides an escape for Circe Berman, who tames her personal demons by writing about the problems of adolescents.

Throughout the novel, Vonnegut demonstrates his mastery of storytelling techniques. As a student of anthropology at the University of Chicago, he wrote a master's thesis analyzing the structure of folk tales, and he put his knowledge of the form to good use in *Bluebeard* (for Vonnegut's recollections of his thesis, see *Palm Sunday* 285–88). Dan Gregory's story of learning to counterfeit Russian banknotes is a perfect counterfeit of a folk tale. It features the familiar characters of the cruel master and his earnest and gifted apprentice. Like many folk tales, the plot repeats itself three times, as Gregory creates a counterfeit and his master rejects it. The repetition sets readers up for the final twist, when Gregory fools his master and proves his superiority as an artist. Vonnegut's study of folk tales taught him that this structure has undeniable appeal, even though it bears little resemblance to the world most people live in. Circe Berman, who wants her books to be realistic, runs into a problem when she begins writing about working-class adolescents who live in a beach resort that is overrun by rich kids in the summer. Her storytelling instincts tell her that readers would enjoy a story about a poor girl who falls in love with a rich boy, but as Slazinger points out, that story is so out of touch with contemporary life that you will not "even see [it] in the *movies* anymore" (29). Writers face a dilemma: How can they be true to their own vision of the world and still appeal to a large audience? Many literary critics, like the art critics discussed earlier, would say that it is impossible to create serious works of literature that are also popular with readers. Vonnegut has walked a tightrope between literature and popular fiction for his entire career, and while it has brought him scorn from critics who treat his performance like a circus stunt, his novels have gotten average people thinking about serious issues that are rarely discussed in the popular media. In *Bluebeard*, he argues that the primary function of art is to communicate with others and that artists must use all of the techniques at their disposal to reach as wide an audience as possible.

Bluebeard returns to one of Vonnegut's favorite themes, the loss of the traditional extended family and the loneliness that Americans endure in spite of the "artificial extended families" they create to fill the void (195). The Armenian genocide put an abrupt and dramatic end to Rabo Karabekian's traditional extended family, but the mundane pressures of modern life are powerful enough to break up most families. *Bluebeard* asks readers to think about what life was like when small groups of people, most of whom were related by blood, lived in the same place for generations. After a while, the place became as sacred to them as Mount Ararat is to the Armenians. They took care of one another's physical needs, but more importantly, they provided the companionship that all human beings crave. Sharing the same stories and the same experiences, they understood one another as modern people so rarely do. Vonnegut's nostalgia for the traditional extended family comes from the dispersal of his own family after World War II. He provides a glimpse of one intact American family, the Karpinskis, who have been farming on Long Island for three generations, but most of the novel deals with the harmful effects brought on by the loss of extended families. As Karabekian's immigrant mother soon recognizes, "The most pervasive American disease [is] loneliness" (54). Rabo Karabekian, Circe Berman, and Paul Slazinger all suffer from almost unbearable loneliness, and the search for companionship shapes their lives. Karabekian refuses promotions during the war so that he can remain with his "happy family" of painters, but when the war is over, he loses touch with them. Karabekian admits that he "bought" his next "big family," the Abstract Expressionist painters whom he supported after the war (49). But if Karabekian is so desperate for a family, why does he not pay more attention to his own wife and sons? *Bluebeard* suggests that the modern nuclear family is no substitute for the traditional extended family, simply because it is not big enough to meet the full range of emotional needs that adults have. Karabekian's wife Dorothy does not understand his obsession with painting, and she has no interest in talking about it. He is so out of touch with her concerns that readers never get a clear picture of what she wants. Circe Berman enters Karabekian's life in order to help him, but she is also trying to cobble together an artificial family of her own to cope with the loss of her husband. Paul Slazinger is so starved for friendship that he practically lives at Karabekian's house, barely surviving on a steady diet of quiet companionship from a man he does not even like. Loneliness has prompted Americans to create a whole host of artificial extended families, but they do not provide all the emotional nourishment that people crave. In the terminology that Vonnegut created in *Cat's Cradle*, they are granfalloons, "proud and meaningless associations of human beings" (*Wampeters, Foma & Granfalloons* xiii). After trying to improve his chances of employment during the Depression by building his vocabulary and learning to speak like the graduate of an Ivy League university, Karabekian realizes that "the real treasure the great universities offered was a lifelong membership in a respected artificial family" (195). Membership in such a family conveys prestige and helps employment prospects, but it does not solve the persistent problem of loneliness. After all, Slazinger is "a Harvard man," but this distinction provides little consolation (100). Many people feel alienated from others and from the world around them because they are no longer part of extended families with a shared history. Vonnegut points out that alienation is not only dangerous to their mental health, but to the health and well being of others. Because they feel no special connection to a particular place, Americans are willing to exploit the land for their own profit. Because they lack meaningful connections to other people, they consider them "sub-human aborigines" who exist only to be exploited (190). In this way, Vonnegut connects the very personal disease of loneliness to America's larger social problems, suggesting that until we realize that we are all one big family, there is little hope that we can solve these problems.

A FEMINIST READING

The origins of feminism are often traced back to Mary Wollstonecraft's 1792 book *A Vindication of the Rights of Women*. Wollstonecraft pointed out that men dominated society and decided what roles women were allowed to play. She argued that women must reject the common assumption that they were inferior to men and define their own roles in society. Feminist literary criticism began with Virginia Woolf's influential book *A Room of One's Own*, published in 1919. Woolf was one of the greatest novelists of the twentieth century, and with *A Room of One's Own* she proved that she was also a profound social critic. In order to show how male-dominated society stifles the intellectual and artistic talents of woman, she asks what would have happened if Shakespeare had a sister who was equally gifted? Woolf answers that she would have been denied an education because she was a woman. She could not have found employment outside the home, and without money, she never could have afforded a room of her own, where she would have the time and solitude for thinking and writing. Woolf argues that this talented woman would have ended her days alone, with her gifts unrecognized, because male-dominated society refuses to acknowledge that women are the intellectual and artistic equals of men. Only if women reject this false notion of inferiority can they establish a place for themselves in society that will allow them to develop their talents. Woolf ends on a hopeful note, predicting that women will assert their equality and create a literature worthy of Shakespeare's sister.

More recent feminist critics have analyzed the stereotypical roles that male writers have assigned to women. Literary critics Sandra M. Gilbert and Susan Gubar identified two principal images of women that dominated nineteenth-century literature in their influential book *The Madwoman in the Attic: The Woman Writer and the Nineteenth-Century Literary Imagination*, published in 1979. According to Gilbert and Gubar, women are depicted either as "the angel in the house" or "the madwoman in the attic." If they conform to male expectations and spend their lives caring for their husbands and children with no thought of their own desires, women are angels, but if they reject this role, they are considered crazy and are shut off from the rest of society, like a madwoman locked up in the attic. Feminist critics often re-examine the works of well-known male writers to expose these stereotypes and demonstrate how they perpetuate harmful ideas about what it means to be a woman.

Feminist critics would find little to praise and much to condemn in Vonnegut's earlier novels, but in *Bluebeard*, he seems determined to make amends for the degrading stereotypes of women that abound in his best-known works. In Vonnegut's earlier fiction, mothers tend to be madwomen rather than angels, and Vonnegut dwells on the corrosive effects of their insanity on their sons rather than exploring the causes of their mental illness. In *Bluebeard*, however, Karabekian's mother is a shrewd observer of American society and much better adjusted than her bitter husband. Many women in Vonnegut's earlier fiction are little more than sexual objects for male characters to lust after. Mona Aamons in *Cat's Cradle* and Montana Wildhack in *Slaughterhouse-Five* are obvious examples, but the Noth sisters in *Mother Night* demonstrate how beauty and sexuality often obscure all other aspects of Vonnegut's female characters. Because they resemble each other physically, Howard W. Campbell, Jr., finds it easy to treat them as if they were the same woman. The roles open to women in Vonnegut's fiction through the 1970s mirror the roles they were expected to play in society at large. Karabekian's father summarizes the possibilities as he speculates on Marilee Kemp's real role in

Gregory's household, "maybe his cook, maybe his cleaning woman, maybe his whore" (59).

In Vonnegut's previous fiction, women were often foils for men, but in *Bluebeard*, Karabekian makes both Marilee Kemp and Circe Berman look good by comparison. Both of the women have the supposedly male qualities that Karabekian so obviously lacks. They are ambitious, intelligent, perceptive, resolute, forceful, opinionated, and articulate, all qualities that are highly valued when possessed by men, but that are sometimes considered inappropriate for women. Karabekian, on the other hand, is a passive man who has given up on life. As a pair, he and Circe Berman call to mind Paul and Anita Proteus from Vonnegut's first novel *Player Piano*, which was published in 1952 (see chapter 3 of this volume). While Paul, like Karabekian, believes that his best days are behind him, his wife Anita is creative and ambitious. However, in the social context of the early 1950s, she has no outlet for her ambition or her creativity and she ends up frustrated and crazy, not quite a madwoman in an attic, but trapped in a loveless second marriage to the most despicable character in the book. Circe Berman, on the other hand, is an independent, creative woman with not just a room but a whole house of her own and an impressive record of publication behind her. Thanks in large part to the feminist movement of the 1960s and 1970s, she has opportunities that were not available to Anita three decades earlier, and she uses them to fulfill the promise that lay dormant in Shakespeare's sister.

When Marilee Kemp is first introduced, she seems destined to take her place among the ranks of the brainless sexual objects that are so prevalent in Vonnegut's earlier novels. She is described as a "showgirl," calling to mind the "go-go girl" Lily in *Slaughterhouse-Five*, who is no more than a sign of her aged husband's continuing virility. Furthermore, Marilee's rags-to-riches story follows the broad outlines of the Cinderella tale, in which the oppressed woman is saved by the dashing prince. In the classic tale, Cinderella is the very model of the "angel in the house," cleaning and cooking for her abusive stepmother and stepsisters. The "happy ending" teaches women that they cannot achieve happiness on their own, but only through marriage to the man of their dreams. In *Bluebeard*, Vonnegut rewrites the Cinderella story so that Marilee saves herself, after her two "princes," Dan Gregory and Count Bruno Portomaggiore, turn out to be less than ideal husbands. Although Gregory saves her from the stage manager of the Ziegfeld follies, who made her part of his "stable of whores," he soon becomes abusive, and Marilee learns that all she can expect from him is a place to live (235). Her letters to Karabekian help her realize that the key to happiness lies within and that she must take control of her own life. Becoming a writer transforms her from an object to a subject, as she begins to look at the world from her own point of view rather than accept the vision of the world handed to her by a male-dominated society. The count she later marries is closer to the ideal of the prince because he respects her, but only after his death is Marilee free to write her own happy ending to her amazing story. She sells her husband's enormous collection of male homosexual pornography and distributes the money among women who were injured during the war. Then she makes her own fortune in the male-dominated business world by becoming the largest Sony distributor in all of Europe. She has learned that, far from needing a man to save her, she is better off without men, whom she regards as "not only useless and idiotic, but downright dangerous" (244).

Bluebeard clearly stands apart from Vonnegut's other novels in terms of its characterization of women. Like Rabo Karabekian, Vonnegut seems to be trying to make sense of the profound changes in American society that have occurred in his lifetime. The feminist movement made it impossible for a thinking man to continue to denigrate women by forcing them into stereotyped roles. Vonnegut responded to the challenge by creating two of his best-developed and most interesting characters, both of them women. Although *Slaughterhouse-Five* is a great anti-war novel, it has very little to say about the price women pay when their men go off to war. *Bluebeard* shows that from a woman's point of view, war is the ultimate form of male aggression against women and that until women are in positions of power, there is little hope for a better world. The title of Rabo Karabekian's final painting would also make a good subtitle for this Vonnegut novel: "Now It's the Women's Turn" (303).

Bibliography

Note: Page numbers in the text refer to the Delta/Dell paperback editions of Vonnegut's works.

WORKS BY KURT VONNEGUT

Novels (in chronological order)

Player Piano. New York: Charles Scribner's Sons, 1952, 1980.
The Sirens of Titan. New York: Dell, 1959, 1998.
Mother Night. Greenwich, CT: Fawcett, 1961, 1999.
Cat's Cradle. New York: Holt, Rinehart and Winston, 1963, 1998.
God Bless You, Mr. Rosewater. New York: Holt, Rinehart and Winston, 1965, 1998.
Slaughterhouse-Five. New York: Delacorte Press/Seymour Lawrence, 1969, 1999.
Breakfast of Champions. New York: Delacorte Press/Seymour Lawrence, 1973, 1999.
Slapstick. New York: Delacorte Press/Seymour Lawrence, 1976, 1999.
Jailbird. New York: Delacorte Press/Seymour Lawrence, 1979, 1999.
Deadeye Dick. New York: Delacorte Press/Seymour Lawrence, 1982, 1999.
Galapagos. New York: Delacorte Press/Seymour Lawrence, 1985, 1999.
Bluebeard. New York: Delacorte Press, 1987, 1999.
Hocus Pocus. New York: Putnam, 1990.
Timequake. New York: Putnam, 1997.

Other Works by Vonnegut

Fiction

Bagombo Snuff Box: Uncollected Short Fiction. New York: Putnam, 1997.
Between Time and Timbuktu. New York: Delacorte Press/Seymour Lawrence, 1972.
Canary in a Cat House. Greenwich, CT: Gold Medal Books, 1961.
God Bless You, Dr. Kevorkian. New York: Seven Stories Press, 1999.
Happy Birthday, Wanda June. New York: Delacorte Press/Seymour Lawrence, 1970.
Welcome to the Monkey House. New York: Delacorte Press/Seymour Lawrence, 1968, 1998.

Nonfiction

Fates Worse than Death: An Autobiographical Collage of the 1980s. New York: Putnam, 1991.
Palm Sunday: An Autobiographical Collage. New York: Delacorte Press/Seymour Lawrence, 1981, 1999.
Wampeters, Foma & Granfalloons: Opinions. New York: Delacorte Press/Seymour Lawrence, 1974, 1999.

INTERVIEWS WITH VONNEGUT

Abel, David. "So It Goes for Vonnegut." *The Boston Globe* 5 May 2001: A1, A11.
Allen, William Rodney. *Conversations with Kurt Vonnegut.* Jackson: University of Mississippi Press, 1999.
Bryan, C.D.B. "Kurt Vonnegut, Head Bokononist." *New York Times Book Review* 6 April 1969: 2, 25.
Reed, Peter J., and Marc Leeds, eds. *The Vonnegut Chronicles: Interviews and Essays.* Westport, CT: Greenwood Press, 1996.
Roloff, Lee. "Kurt Vonnegut on Stage at the Steppenwolf Theater, Chicago." *TriQuarterly* 103(Fall 1998): 17–29.
Todd, Richard. "The Masks of Kurt Vonnegut, Jr." *New York Times Magazine* 24 January 1971: 16–17, 19, 22, 24, 26, 30–31.

GENERAL CRITICISM

Allen, William Rodney. *Understanding Kurt Vonnegut.* Columbia: University of South Carolina Press, 1991.
Bloom, Harold, ed. *Modern Critical Views: Kurt Vonnegut.* Philadelphia, PA: Chelsea House, 2000.
Boon, Kevin A. *Chaos Theory and the Interpretation of Literary Texts: The Case of*

Kurt Vonnegut. Studies in American Literature, vol 27. Lewiston, NY: Edwin Mellen Press, 1997.

Broer, Lawrence R. *Sanity Plea: Schizophrenia in the Novels of Kurt Vonnegut*. Ann Arbor, MI: UMI Research Press, 1989.

Fiedler, Leslie A. "The Divine Stupidity of Kurt Vonnegut." *Esquire*, September 1970: 195–97, 199–200, 202–4.

Giannone, Richard. *Vonnegut: A Preface to His Novels*. Port Washington, NY: Kennikat, 1977.

Goldsmith, David H. *Kurt Vonnegut: Fantasist of Fire and Ice*. Bowling Green, KY: Bowling Green University Popular Press, 1972.

Hipkiss, Robert A. *The American Absurd: Pynchon, Vonnegut, and Barth*. Port Washington, NY: National University Publications/Associated Faculty Press, 1984.

Hoffman, Thomas P. "The Theme of Mechanization in *Player Piano*." In *Clockwork Worlds: Mechanized Environments in SF*, edited by Richard P. Erlich and Thomas P. Dunn. Westport CT: Greenwood Press, 1983.

Hume, Kathryn. "The Heraclitean Cosmos of Kurt Vonnegut." *Papers on Language and Literature* 18 (1982): 204–24.

———. "Kurt Vonnegut and the Myths and Symbols of Meaning." *Texas Studies in Literature and Language* 24 (1982): 429–47.

Klinkowitz, Jerome. *Kurt Vonnegut*. London: Methuen, 1982.

———. *Slaughterhouse-Five: Reforming the Novel and the World*. Boston: Twayne Publishers, 1990.

———. *Vonnegut in Fact: The Public Spokesmanship of Personal Fiction*. Columbia: University of South Carolina Press, 1998.

Klinkowitz, Jerome, and Donald L. Lawler, eds. *Vonnegut in America*. New York: Delacorte Press/Seymour Lawrence, 1977.

Klinkowitz, Jerome, and John Somer, eds. *The Vonnegut Statement*. New York: Delacorte/Seymour Lawrence, 1973.

Leeds, Marc. *The Vonnegut Encyclopedia: An Authorized Compendium*. Westport, CT: Greenwood Press, 1995.

Leeds, Marc, and Peter J. Reed, eds. *Kurt Vonnegut: Images and Representations*. Westport, CT: Greenwood Press, 2000.

Lundquist, James. *Kurt Vonnegut*. New York: Ungar, 1977.

Merrill, Robert, ed. *Critical Essays on Kurt Vonnegut*. Boston: G. K. Hall, 1990.

Morse, Donald E. *Kurt Vonnegut*. San Bernadino, CA: The Borgo Press, 1992.

Mustazza, Leonard. *Forever Pursuing Genesis: The Myth of Eden in the Novels of Kurt Vonnegut*. Lewisburg, PA: Bucknell University Press, 1990.

Mustazza, Leonard, ed. *The Critical Response to Kurt Vonnegut*. Westport, CT: Greenwood Press, 1994.

Pettersson, Bo. *The World According to Kurt Vonnegut: Moral Paradox and Narrative Form*. Åbo, Finland: Åbo Akademi University Press, 1994.

Pierrat, Asa B., Julie Huffman-Klinkowitz, and Jerome Klinkowitz. *Kurt Vonnegut: A Comprehensive Bibliography*. Hamden, CT: Archon, 1987.

Reed, Peter J. *Kurt Vonnegut, Jr.* New York: Warner, 1972.

————. *The Short Fiction of Kurt Vonnegut.* Westport, CT: Greenwood Press, 1997.

Reed, Peter J., and Marc Leeds, eds. *The Vonnegut Chronicles: Interviews and Essays.* Westport, CT: Greenwood Press, 1996.

Scholes, Robert. *Fabulation and Metafiction.* Chicago: University of Illinois Press, 1979.

Tanner, Tony. *City of Words: American Fiction 1950–1970.* New York: Harper and Row, 1971.

REVIEWS AND CRITICISM

Player Piano

Chicago Sunday Tribune, 24 August 1952: 2.
Fantasy and Science Fiction, November 1966: 2.
Library Journal, August 1952: 1303.
New Republic, 18 August 1952: 19.
New Yorker, 16 August 1952: 88.
Saturday Review, 30 August 1952: 11.
Saturday Review, 14 May 1966: 44.

The Sirens of Titan

Book World, 26 July 1981: 6.
Observer, 2 November 1975: 29.
Times Literary Supplement, 15 June 1967: 543.

Mother Night

Choice, Summer, 1966: 524.
Harper's, May 1966: 103.
Psychology Today, August 1974: 20.
Saturday Review, 14 May 1966: 44.
Time, 29 April 1966: 122.

Cat's Cradle

Best Sellers (Vol. 25), 1 October 1965: 274.
New York Times Book Review, 2 June 1963: 20.
Observer, 22 August 1965: 21.
Spectator, 2 August 1963: 158–59.
Thought (Vol. 56), March 1981: 63.

God Bless You, Mr. Rosewater

Fantasy and Science Fiction, 27 July 1965: 78–83.
Life, 9 April 1965: 6, 10.
New Yorker, 15 May 1965: 216.
New York Times, 9 April 1965: 35M.
New York Times Book Review, 25 April 1965: 41.
Time, 7 May 1965: 112–14.
Times Literary Supplement, 11 November 1965: 1007.

Slaughterhouse-Five

Atlantic, April 1969: 146.
Life, 21 March 1969: 9.
Nation, 9 June 1969: 736.
New Republic, 26 April 1969: 33–35.
Newsweek, 14 April 1969: 122.
New Yorker, 17 May 1969: 145.
New York Review of Books, 2 July 1970: 7–8.
New York Times Book Review, 6 April 1969: 1, 23.
Saturday Review, 29 March 1969: 25.
Time, 11 April 1969: 106.

Bluebeard

Book World (Vol. 17), 4 October 1987: 9.
Books, April 1988: 16.
Los Angeles Times Book Review, 4 October 1987: 10.
North American Review, March 1988: 65–67.
Time, 28 September 1987: 67.
The Times Literary Supplement, 29 April 1988: 470.

WORKS OF GENERAL INTEREST

Bressler, Charles E. *Literary Criticism: An Introduction to Theory and Practice*. 2nd
    ed. Upper Saddle River, NJ: Prentice Hall, 1999.
Eichmann, Adolph. "I Transported Them . . . to the Butcher." *Life* 49:22 (1960):
    19–25, 101–112.
———. "To Sum It All Up, I Regret Nothing." *Life* 49:23 (1960): 146–154.
Gilbert, Sandra M., and Susan Gubar. *The Madwoman in the Attic: The Woman
    Writer and the Nineteenth-Century Literary Imagination*. New Haven, CT:
    Yale University Press, 1979.
Hadas, Moses, ed. *The Complete Plays of Aristophanes*. New York: Bantam, 1962.
Halberstam, David. *The Fifties*. New York: Fawcett, 1993.

Keats, John. *Poems and Selected Letters*. Edited by Carlos Baker. New York: Bantam, 1962.

Melville, Herman. *Moby Dick*. (1851). Boston: Houghton Mifflin, 1956.

Morgan, Edward P. *The 60s Experience: Hard Lessons about Modern America*. Philadelphia, PA: Temple University Press, 1991.

Orwell, George. *1984*. New York: New American Library, 1989.

———. *Animal Farm*. New York: Plume/Harcourt Brace, 1996.

———. "Politics and the English Language." In *The Collected Essays, Journalism, and Letters of George Orwell*, edited by Sonia Orwell and Ian Angus. New York: Harcourt, Brace & World, 1968.

Taylor, Telford. Review of *The Rise and Fall of the Third Reich: A History of Nazi Germany* by William L. Shirer. *Saturday Review*, 15 October 1960: 23–24.

Wollstonecraft, Mary. *A Vindication of the Rights of Women*. (1792). New York: Source Book Press, 1971.

Woolf, Virginia. *A Room of One's Own*. (1919). New York: Cambridge University Press, 1995.

Index

About the Author

THOMAS F. MARVIN is Assistant Professor of English and American Studies at Indiana University Purdue University Indianapolis. He has published articles on African-American literature and music in both *American Literature* and *African American Review*.

Critical Companions to Popular Contemporary Writers
First Series—*also available on CD-ROM*

V. C. Andrews
  by E. D. Huntley

Tom Clancy
  by Helen S. Garson

Mary Higgins Clark
  by Linda C. Pelzer

Arthur C. Clarke
  by Robin Anne Reid

James Clavell
  by Gina Macdonald

Pat Conroy
  by Landon C. Burns

Robin Cook
  by Lorena Laura Stookey

Michael Crichton
  by Elizabeth A. Trembley

Howard Fast
  by Andrew Macdonald

Ken Follett
  by Richard C. Turner

John Grisham
  by Mary Beth Pringle

James Herriot
  by Michael J. Rossi

Tony Hillerman
  by John M. Reilly

John Jakes
  by Mary Ellen Jones

Stephen King
  by Sharon A. Russell

Dean Koontz
  by Joan G. Kotker

Robert Ludlum
  by Gina Macdonald

Anne McCaffrey
  by Robin Roberts

Colleen McCullough
  by Mary Jean DeMarr

James A. Michener
  by Marilyn S. Severson

Anne Rice
  by Jennifer Smith

Tom Robbins
  *by Catherine E. Hoyser and
  Lorena Laura Stookey*

John Saul
  by Paul Bail

Erich Segal
  by Linda C. Pelzer

Gore Vidal
  *by Susan Baker and
  Curtis S. Gibson*